Curricular Landscapes, Democratic Vistas

Curricular Landscapes, Democratic Vistas

TRANSFORMATIVE LEADERSHIP IN HIGHER EDUCATION

William G. Tierney

PRAEGER

New York
Westport, Connecticut
London

Library of Congress Cataloging-in-Publication Data

Tierney, William G.
    Curricular landscapes, democratic vistas : transformative
leadership in higher education / William G. Tierney.
       p.   cm.
    Bibliography: p.
    Includes index.
    ISBN 0–275–93371–7 (alk. paper)
    1. Universities and colleges—United States—Curricula—Case
studies. 2. Universities and colleges—United States—
Administration—Case studies   I. Title.
LB2361.5.T54   1989
378.1'99'0973—dc20   89–33972

Copyright © 1989 by William G. Tierney

Library of Congress Catalog Card Number: 89–33972
ISBN: 0–275–93371–7

First published in 1989

Praeger Publishers, One Madison Avenue, New York, NY 10010
A division of Greenwood Press, Inc.

Printed in the United States of America

The paper used in this book complies with the
Permanent Paper Standard issued by the National
Information Standards Organization (Z39.48–1984).

10 9 8 7 6 5 4 3 2 1

AMERICA THE BEAUTIFUL

O beautiful for spacious skies
   For amber waves of grain,
For purple mountain majesties
   Above the fruited plain!
   America! America!
God shed His grace on thee
And crown thy good with brotherhood
   From sea to shining sea!

O beautiful for pilgrim feet
   Whose stern, impassioned stress,
A thoroughfare for freedom beat
   Across the wilderness!
   America! America!
God mend thine every flaw,
Confirm thy soul in self-control,
   Thy liberty in law!

O beautiful for heroes proved
   In liberating strife,
Who more than self their country loved
   And mercy more than life!
   America! America!
May God thy gold refine,
Till all success be nobleness
   And every gain divine!

O beautiful for patriot dream
   That sees beyond the years,
Thine alabaster cities gleam
   Undimmed by human tears!
   America! America!
God shed His grace on thee
And crown thy good with brotherhood
   From sea to shining sea!

                                 Katharine Lee Bates

Contents

Part IV: Transformative Leadership

Preface

Without the encouragement of colleagues and friends at the Center for the Study of Higher Education at Penn State University this book would have been impossible. Sally Kelley arranged the site visits, typed and proofread this manuscript and, along with Marilyn Downing and Beverly Ladrido, helped create a positive working environment at the Center. My research assistant, Beth Jones, helped compile the bibliography and ensure the accuracy of the text. Kay Moore, then Director of the Center for the Study of Higher Education at Penn State, and now at Michigan State, was instrumental in the completion of this book. Kay provided criticism and feedback on earlier drafts that helped me reformulate my ideas. Penn State's loss is Michigan State's gain. Finally, the generous support of Ralph Lundgren and the Lilly Endowment provided me with the funding to conduct the research that has resulted in this book. Needless to say, the ideas in this work reflect my own notions about the curriculum.

I have also been fortunate in the sites for these case studies, the individuals interviewed and, most especially, the institutional liaisons who agreed to help arrange my visits during the academic year 1987–88. In virtually all instances hardworking individuals—administrators, faculty, staff, students, and parents—donated their time to provide the data that make up this book.

Yet when I write I do not only need helpful colleagues, willing respondents, and a gracious foundation; I also need friendship and intellectual stimulation. Again, I am very fortunate. Intellectually, the works of Henry Giroux and Daniel McLaughlin have been of tremendous benefit. As will be evident, Giroux's writing has had an impact on my thinking about the curriculum in higher education. As an educator at Rock Point School on the Navajo Reservation, Dan McLaughlin has shown me by example how theory informs practice.

Nancy Leimbacher, Claire Martin, Kim Trimble, Ellen Chaffee, Fred Weaver, Roger Platizky, and Barry Weiss offered me their help, advice, humor, and support when I most often needed it. I am in their debt. In a small way, I hope the ideas in this book that speak to reinstilling a democratic vista on America's campuses, repay these friends and colleagues.

Introduction

In 1893 the author of *America the Beautiful*, Katharine Lee Bates, joined an expedition in a prairie wagon to the 14,110-foot summit of Pikes Peak. "Our sojourn on the peak remains in memory hardly more than one ecstatic gaze," she wrote. "As I was looking out over the sealike expanse of fertile country spreading away so far under those ample skies, the opening lines of the hymn floated into my mind" (Burgess, 1952, p. 102).

Anyone who has climbed the Rocky Mountains of Colorado understands how Bates could have written those words. After the labor of winding one's way up mountain trails, over huge boulders and thin sandlike scree one is afforded an incomparable view.

In July of 1987, a friend and I climbed Wilson Peak in the southwestern corner of Colorado. Even at the height of summer, a Colorado morning in the high Rockies begins with a light layer of frost that covers the earth. Although the climb up Wilson Peak begins gradually through magnificent fields of columbine, bluebells, Indian paintbrush, and ponderosa pine, after two miles the trail arches abruptly upward until Navajo Lake. On a cloudless day the water glistens in a brilliance that makes it appear as if it were a mirror. Unencumbered by the symbols of the modern world, the lake enfolds its surroundings in panoramic splendor. On the northwest corner of the lake the San Miguel Mountains are reflected; the southern half of the lake faces the open basin toward Mt. Dolores and Utah.

Beyond the lake to the north is the footpath to the summit. The trail evaporates over the last mile of the hike, and climbers must scramble over boulders to reach the peak. Presumably I am not the only one whose legs shake as a loose rock rumbles out from below and whose hands cling to the cliff in the hope of not following the cascade down the mountain. To reach the summit we must physically pull ourselves upward beyond the ridge and onto the peak. A shock of surprise follows: everywhere we look, snowcapped mountains can be seen. It is as if we have ascended into the clouds and can see all of America "from sea to shining sea."

Less than a day's drive from Wilson Peak in northwestern New Mexico is Chaco Canyon, center of one of the oldest civilizations in the Americas—the Anasazi. A different kind of sensibility comes over visitors to the canyon. Rather than feeling that we have reached the heavens, the quiet of the canyon and the knowledge that people lived here over a thousand years ago forces us to reflect on our history and relationship to the earth. A sense of spirituality pervades virtually all parts of the canyon.

In the depth of summer, even the late evenings are hot; at midday the sun shines so intensely that heat waves shimmer in the distance. Ancient ruins stand magnificently throughout the landscape. Walking down one trail or another, one commonly finds arrowheads or faded chips of pottery from the reign of the Anasazi in 500 AD. Unearthed kivas, garden plots, and pueblos provide a wealth of evidence about the civilizations that once walked here. Archaeologists have estimated that 6,000 people lived in 400 settlements in the early 12th century; visible arts, architecture, ceramics, and advanced agricultural techniques attest to the resonance of early Chacoan culture (Lister & Lister, 1981).

Midnight in the desert canyon affords a silence and solemnity that we rarely find elsewhere. Miles from city lights and the noises of modern civilization, the stars in the sky light the desert in a soft brilliance that etches the formations of the surrounding mountains and pueblos. The echo of silence can be deafening to those of us who are accustomed to the constant background noises of the city.

Mountains and canyons. Landscapes and vistas. Pikes Peak and Chaco Canyon speak to both the unity and the distinctive nature of America's democracy. Atop the mountain at midday we behold the "sealike expanse of fertile country," that makes up the United States. The silence of the canyon at midnight offers us the opportunity to reflect on our own lives.

Looking out on America from mountaintops and looking backward toward the roots of our civilization frame this book's content. The landscape of the curriculum of the seven institutions that I studied during 1987–88 also speaks about the archaeology of our civilization, our conception of who we are, and, ultimately, what kind of society we want to be in the twenty-first century.

This book has four parts. As mountain climbers usually have an idea about which trail they will use to reach a summit, Part I provides readers with a conceptual map of the terrain we will encounter. First curricular, and then cultural theories sketch the landscape to be covered. Parts II and III delve into the archaeology of the curriculum at the seven institutions. Part II provides readers with a perspective on how the participants in the seven colleges and universities view different curricular concepts. Part III portrays how the individuals view one another's actions about the curriculum. As I will demonstrate, the curriculum often becomes contested terrain because of the cultural constructions different groups develop about one another and toward the curriculum. Part IV offers an interpretation and analysis of the different curricular formations of the seven institutions and concludes with a discussion of how organizational participants might assume the role of transformative leaders who create new curricular paths and directions for their institutions.

The institutions to be discussed will be referred to as:

- Cutting Edge College (CEC)
- Working-Class State College (WCSC)
- Christian University (CU)
- Classics College (CC)
- Entrepreneurial College (EC)
- Testimony State College (TSC)
- Women's College (WC)

"College," "university," and "institution" will be used interchangeably.

Terms such as "Faculty Advisory Committee" and "Curriculum Affairs Committee" are also generic.

I

A Conceptual Map of the Terrain

The cocks of dawn would catch us trying to give order to the chain of many chance events that had made absurdity possible, and it was obvious that we weren't doing it from an urge to clear up mysteries but because none of us could go on living without an exact knowledge of the place and the mission assigned to us by fate.

Gabriel Garcia Marquez

1

The Curricular Landscape in Higher Education

The impetus for this study derives from two previous works (Tierney, 1988; Chaffee & Tierney, 1988) where I investigated decision making and leadership in higher education. As I undertook and reflected on both works, the organizational participants' confusion about the mission of their institution and the curriculum kept cropping up. The people with whom I spoke appeared at a loss as to how to "manage" the curriculum and what an institutional mission meant in operational terms. Different people defined the curriculum in disparate ways; at different institutions people conceived of what a curricular structure was, and what it should do, in radically divergent manners. On the simplest level, I wanted to conduct a study that looked in depth at the curriculum and the actors involved in it.

On a related level, I have become increasingly concerned about the epistemological premises of much of the conventional research about the curriculum in higher education. The majority of analyses of curricular and organizational theory in higher education operate from similar theoretical premises. Broadly stated, conventional researchers assume: that a theory is a set of lawlike propositions that is empirically testable; that knowledge is objective and capable of being studied from a neutral stance; and, relatedly, that a researcher's values ought not to influence one's findings.

My assumption is that knowledge is socially constructed, which is antithetical to the usual idea that knowledge exists "out there"—external to and independent of the knower. Postsecondary organizations are cultures that embody competing conceptions of reality and what constitutes knowledge. If knowledge is socially constructed, then the methodology used to study the curriculum needs to unearth the multitude of organizational voices in order to understand how knowledge has been constructed, who has constructed it, and what alternative constructions are possible. Since I do not assume that knowledge is objective, then I also must reject the notion that research is value-neutral or external to the researcher; instead, I intend to make explicit my own values and premises about the curriculum.

Accordingly, the purpose of this work is threefold. First, it will offer a different way of thinking and talking about the curriculum in post-secondary education than has been customary. As opposed to discussing whether higher education's curriculum should be formed around the universal truths of Western civilization, it will show how the curriculum is a cultural product which the participants in institutions socially construct. The manner in which the institution defines the curriculum commits the institution to philosophical and ideological choices, whether recognized or not.

Second, this book will consider how an institution's mission and curricula may act as a critical agent for preparing students to participate in and struggle in the democratic public sphere. That is, as a product and producer of an organization's culture, the curriculum is not merely a reflection of the organization and society. Thus discussion is redirected away from the current debate over which facts should be on a cultural literacy test for college graduates, and toward the idea that the organizing principle of a college or university is the principle of diversity. Seen in this light, postsecondary institutions stand for a freedom of inquiry that supports the unhindered assertion, discussion, and development of ideas.

Thus, the proposition is to lay out a schema of postsecondary life that works from the assumption that the unique role of colleges and universities is not merely to socialize students about the eternal verities of Western civilization, but rather to empower students so that they may become centrally involved in the struggle for democracy as we approach the twenty-first century. As opposed to assuming that we should reach a consensus about requirements for curricular issues, such as general education or foreign languages, we will discuss how democracy as an organizing principle helps focus institutional discourse and promote academic freedom.

Finally, strategies will be suggested that administrators and faculty may employ to advance the democratic ideal in their colleges and universities. As opposed to rationalist organizational models of academic life that provide administrative blueprints for success (Bennett, 1983; Tucker, 1984) or theories that speak to administrative inability to create academic change (Cohen & March, 1974), Aronowitz's and Giroux's concept of the "transformative intellectual" (1985) will be utilized as an organizing principle. From this perspective, participants in higher education are neither Weberian experts who define and control organizational reality, nor are they powerless pawns in a game that no one controls. Rather, we will consider how administrators and faculty may rededicate themselves to the values of the intellect and reinforce the democratic imperative in those whom we educate.

Prior to entering the terrain of the seven institutions, it is helpful to take a step back and first briefly consider the curricular landscape in higher education. Current concerns and issues that have been expressed about the curriculum will be pointed out, and how we may locate these concerns in the historical discussion of higher education's curriculum will be considered. Additional questions are also warranted. How does a concern for democracy differ from other curricular approaches? How were the data excavated that account for Parts II and III? By addressing these questions and concerns I will develop a schema of key concepts and issues common to all of the institutions. Finally, a map also is provided for following the routes of the subsequent chapters.

THE CURRENT CURRICULAR CONTEXT OF HIGHER EDUCATION

We live at an opportune time for a discussion about higher education's curriculum and its relationship to democracy. Ninety-five percent of the nation's colleges and universities have recently attempted curricular change (El-Khawas, 1987, p. 3). The stimulus for these attempts at curricular change has been the spate of national reports that have appeared over the last decade. Future historians of American higher education will surely remember the 1980s for the avalanche of reports and books about postsecondary education that called for dramatic changes

(Boyer, 1987; National Governor's Association, 1986; Rudolph, 1985; Newman, 1985; Bennett, 1984; Mortimer, 1984a).

In general, the authors of the reports focused their attention in two directions: problems with the curriculum and managerial problems. The reports often criticized faculty and administrators for failing to enhance the meaning and quality of the undergraduate curriculum. According to the reports, a strong liberal arts or general education component must form the core of the curriculum; too often institutions lacked such a definable core. Inadequate presidential authority over internal affairs and lack of faculty leadership in curricular matters received a special amount of criticism. "The decline" . . . wrote William Bennett, "was caused in part by a failure of nerve and faith on the part of many college faculties and administrators, and persists because of a vacuum in educational leadership" (1984, p. 2).

Faculty are recognized as central to the curricular change process. They are the professional staff charged with designing and delivering undergraduate instruction. Yet, according to the reports, they have neglected their duties. "Central to the troubles and to the solutions are the professors," state the authors of the report by the Association of American Colleges (AAC, 1985, p. 6).

Similarly, academic administrators are charged with initiating change and bringing faculty together toward a common purpose, but the reports suggest that, instead, administrators have tended to emphasize off-campus duties and to foster a myopic view of the institution. The president and other principal academic officers have been criticized for abdicating their roles as major actors in formulating curricular missions for their institutions. Presidents increasingly see themselves as fund-raisers, and academic leaders such as deans have become caught up in the more prosaic day-to-day details that demand increased time and attention (Kerr & Gade, 1987).

The criticism about the curriculum and academic management, although significant for the sheer volume of reports generated, is not new. Gerald Graff notes, "The current attempt to unify the humanities curriculum around some vision of educational fundamentals is only the latest in a long series of such efforts, which have invariably ended in futility" (1988, p. 48). As one reviews the history of American higher education, it is remarkable how often criticism has been made of higher education's curricular offerings and those who manage the curriculum, and yet so much still needs to be done.

In 1828, for example, the writers of the Yale Report struggled to maintain the classical curriculum as it came under attack from revisionists. The authors stated, "We are aware that the system is imperfect: and we cherish the hope, that some of its defects may ere long be remedied" (Conrad, 1985, p. 110). Nicholas Murray Butler, in 1905, spoke about the need for "an end of the idling and dawdling that now characterize so much of American higher education" (Rudolph, 1977, p. 207). "Unless some such demonstration or some such evangelist movement can take place," wrote Robert Maynard Hutchins in 1936, "we shall remain in our confusion; we shall have neither general education nor universities; and we shall continue to disappoint the hopes of our people" (p. 87). In 1967 Daniel Bell penned *Reforming General Education* and said, "It has been suggested that liberal arts education has lost its force . . . that the requirements of early specialization are in the process of transforming the college into a pre-professional school" (Lee, p. 347). Finally, in 1985, the authors of the report for the Association of American Colleges wrote, "As for what passes as a college curriculum, almost anything goes. . . . There is so much confusion . . . that it is no longer possible to be sure why a student should take a particular program of courses" (p. 2).

It is interesting to note how often the language of polemic has been used to advocate curricular change. Words and phrases such as "failure of nerve," "idling," "dawdling," and "confusion" characterize the debate about curricular matters. Consequently, one problem readers encounter with most of the recent reports and much of the previous writing on the curriculum is that proposals often appear either doctrinaire, or so utopian that change is impossible. A Great Books list (Bennett, 1984) that all college students should read is an example of a doctrinaire proposal that often has led to failure. The assumption behind the proposal is usually too narrowly conceived to win widespread faculty support. As Chapter 4 will suggest, faculty conceptions of knowledge vary so widely that the assumption that a set list of books can either be devised or agreed upon is farfetched except in the rarest of instances.

Conversely, the utopian suggestions that administrators substantially increase faculty salaries (Mortimer, 1984a) while at the same time substantially reduce the number of students in the classroom (Boyer, 1987) appear difficult at best to administrators who find it next to impossible to balance budgets in light of increased expenditures and decreased income. Indeed, part of the reason presidents do not attend to the academic side of their institutions is that they are constantly in search of finances to help balance the budget and maintain the physical plant.

The utilization of a discourse of polemic and utopia stems in part from the practice of many current and past writers to reify the curriculum as if it were an identifiable object that is knowable to all individuals without regard to time or place. In general, what the authors have done is to collapse curricular theory and practice in their attempt to answer what a curriculum should be. In their efforts to provide curricular solutions the writers have acted as if there is only one epistemological position about knowledge, and hence, the curriculum. From this perspective, knowledge does exist "out there," external to and independent of the knower. It is as if knowledge is a jigsaw puzzle that can be shaped into multiple pictures; even though different representations can be drawn, the pieces of the puzzle are the same to all of the organizational players. A polemicist such as Bennett may try to persuade us that only one picture should be drawn; a utopian such as Boyer may try to help us fashion the pieces of the puzzle according to our own desires. Nevertheless, Bennett, Boyer, and other conventional researchers still assume that the pieces of knowledge are all the same.

Previous research investigations about the curriculum such as those undertaken by Dressel (1971), Mayhew and Ford (1971) and Bergquist (1977) highlight the problems that occur when we enfold practice into theory and assume that, although there may be different knowledge puzzles, the pieces are the same. Each of the authors has struggled to describe different curricular models. In general, the models relate to the explicit emphases institutions have for the curriculum. For example, Bergquist has combined the work of Dressel, Mayhew and Ford; he has arrived at the following list of curricular models in higher education:

1. Heritage Based: A curriculum designed to inculcate students with a knowledge of the past.
2. Thematic Based: A specific problem (such as the environment) is identified and studied in-depth.
3. Competency Based: Students learn specific skills such as proficiency in language and mathematics.
4. Career Based: The curriculum is designed to prepare students for a specific career.

5. Experience Based: Opportunities are created for the student to learn outside of the classroom.
6. Student Based: The curricular emphasis is on providing students with the opportunities to control what they learn.
7. Values Based: The curriculum emphasizes specific institutional values.
8. Future Based: The institution devises the curricular content with a concern for what students will need in the future.

Bergquist's work is quite helpful in providing one view of a curricular undertaking. The problem with such lists, however, is that we overlook how colleges and universities serve, reproduce, and challenge the social order of the society in which they reside. The implicit assumption remains: there is an objective reality to which all of the models apply. As opposed to investigating how theory operates as a set of filters through which we define and choose what counts as knowledge, Berquist's work and most other previous research about the curriculum assume that knowledge is a given. The institution simply arranges the elements of knowledge according to a particular curricular model.

Yet each of the above curricular models has implicit values that need to be unearthed. A heritage-based model, for example, certainly will have different curricular offerings depending upon whose history and whose culture is included. Similarly, a value-based curriculum will look differently in an organization that adheres to conservative religious mores, and an organization that premises itself on a theology of liberation. The point is that to understand the curriculum we need to go beyond articulating models of curricular formations and move toward an archaeology of the curriculum that unearths the inherent premises and values of the organization. Such an excavation will unveil that different institutions have quite different conceptions of knowledge. In short, not only the terrain will be different, but the manner in which the organizational players interpret and use the landscape will also differ. In this light, the relative importance of one curricular model or another is not critical. No one best curricular model to which all institutions must subscribe will be found. How the organizational participants construct their reality implies that different realities exist. Not only will institutions arrive at different curricular models; the institutions will also begin with differing conceptions of what is knowledge.

My assumption is that to understand the curriculum in higher education we must investigate the organizations in which the curriculum resides; to comprehend the culture of educational organizations we need to employ a theoretical framework that delineates the relationship between the organization and society. By following this line of reasoning I attempt to address the problem that Mayhew and Ford acknowledged at the end of their book, *Changing the Curriculum*: "Higher education today does not have the benefit of a fully developed theory to serve as a guide in curriculum matters, but the hope is that this situation will be remedied before too long a time has passed" (1971, p. 179).

Accordingly, it is proposed that we step back from the fray and consider what is actually taking place on specific college and university campuses. Rather than suggest decontextualized notions of what students ought to know, or offer proposals about what administrators and faculty should do if they had unlimited funding, we will consider the social life of seven institutions and discuss how their missions and curricula are socially created. The social constructions of the institutions then will be linked to the larger issues of democracy and suggestions offered as to how administrators and faculty in the institutions might change their curriculum in light of society's democratic needs for the twenty-first century. We now turn to a discussion of the curriculum from the perspective of recent critics, and from the perspective of the curriculum's relationship to democracy.

DEMOCRACY AND THE CURRICULUM: THE CURRENT DEBATE

In the recent past, with few exceptions, we have not concerned ourselves with fashioning a view of postsecondary institutions as democratic spheres. The overwhelming analyses of educational organizations in the United States have used effectiveness and efficiency both as organizing concepts and as ends in themselves (Foster, 1986). We also find that quantitative studies of effectiveness and efficiency are the major concerns of higher education administrators and researchers (Keller, 1985). For example, a search of the ERIC data base for the years between 1966 and 1985 yields more than 1200 entries for the descriptor "organizational effectiveness" (Krakower, 1985). Restricting the search to a combination of "organizational effectiveness" and "colleges and universities" produces more than 300 entries.

Since 1984 two of the primary research journals in higher education, the *Journal of Higher Education* and the *Review of Higher Education*, have devoted entire issues to the concept of effectiveness and efficiency in higher education. Both federally funded National Centers for the Study of Higher Education have used effectiveness extensively in their analyses of educational dilemmas and issues. And, as noted, authors have penned no fewer than six major reports on quality and effectiveness in higher education in the 1980s. Clearly, the articles, journals, federally funded research activities, and reports have brought national focus to the effectiveness of the undergraduate experience. A reasonable question to ask is why so much discussion has been generated about effectiveness and efficiency, and why so little discussion has occurred abut democracy. Why has our central focus concerned whether the curriculum is effective in its operation? How does a concern for efficiency affect the outcomes we will find in our research?

The situation in which higher education finds itself can be traced: (a) to a backlash against the reforms made in the 1960s, (b) to the fundamental problems generated by declining resources in the late 1970s and 1980s, and (c) to the changed perceptions of key constituencies in higher education about the purpose of higher education, and of consequence, the curriculum.

In support of the revisionist views of the 1960s Jeffrey Holland reflects:

The late sixties and early seventies were the darkest hours in the history of American higher education, a dark night of the institutional soul from which we have not yet and may not ever fully recover. In their disdain for standards and their demand for relevance, our cultural continuity was eroded, and any institutional sense of morality regarding a student's course work, conversation, conduct or sexual conquest was obliterated. . . . Now in the eighties, we are trying to pick up the pieces. (1985, p. 58)

Holland's lament is widespread, as witness Allan Bloom, whose *The Closing of the American Mind* has become the most popular book about higher education in the 1980s. As with Holland, Bloom decries the loss of quality in American higher education. Bloom's thesis is that we are no longer effective at educating our young; we have lost our competitive edge and our understanding of what it means to be liberally educated because of the excesses of the 1960s.

Summing up the cause of the problem succinctly in the foreword to Bloom's book, Saul Bellow writes, "The university has become in-

undated and saturated with the backflow of society's 'problems' ''
(1987, p. 18). As one reads the book it becomes clear that the ''backflow'' refers to previously underrepresented constituencies in higher
education such as African Americans and women. It is these people,
Bloom argues, whose demands for relevance have caused the curriculum
to become watered down and saturated with trivial texts at the expense
of the classical curriculum.

Thus, educational quality and effectiveness have been placed in opposition to educational access. For example, the AAC report states:

As laudable as it may be as an ideal, the widening of access also has contributed
to the confusions that have beset the baccalaureate experience. The tension
between democratic values and the effort to maintain standards for an undergraduate education can be creative, but too often numbers and political considerations have prevailed over quality. (1985, p. 5)

The report prepared by the Commission for Educational Quality
states:

The issue of access has dominated higher education since the 1960's. Quality
became a secondary concern, in part because the early covenant did not specify
standards for the programs to which access should be provided . . . as a way of
extending access to all levels of higher education, faculty and administrators
lowered standards for courses, student promotion, and graduation. (1985, p. 2)

The critics argue that the decline of the undergraduate curriculum is
at the heart of higher education's problems. They feel that fads and
fashions, the demands of popularity and success, enter where wisdom
and experience should prevail. Former Secretary of Education Bennett
and others have likened college courses ''to a self-service cafeteria.''
They argue that higher education has become a supermarket where
students are shoppers and professors are merchants of learning.

We see the degree to which students have become consumers who
are dominated by labor market considerations by the proliferation of
professional and technical courses and the concomitant decline in the
humanities and social sciences. The catchword of the 1960s—relevance—has remained important, but instead of a curriculum that is
relevant to fomenting democracy, students seek courses that are relevant
to the marketplace.

The critics cite alarming statistics: Scores in most categories of the

Graduate Record Examination have declined between 1964 and 1982; half of the students who start college with the intention of getting a bachelor's degree drop out before finishing; one of eight very able high school seniors chooses not to attend college. Increasing numbers of students in colleges choose narrow vocational specialties. Steep declines in enrollment have occurred in the physical sciences, biological sciences, social sciences and, of course, the humanities. Increasing requirements in professional fields have prevented students from obtaining a broad liberal arts background; the liberal arts have become service programs for the professions.

The changes in emphases from the 1960s to the present day have created nightmarish dilemmas for administrators who struggle to respond to the customer. Viewing different cadres of students as "markets," admissions programs have tried to capture their share of an audience in order to hold enrollments steady against decline in the traditional age group. Part-time students, returning adult students, and international students have all become critical markets for institutions to capture. Night courses, "weekend colleges," and outreach programs into the business community are examples of adaptive strategies administrators have called upon to satisfy consumer preferences.

Students who view themselves as consumers have chosen to attend institutions where "relevant" courses in business, computer science, and the like take precedence over Shakespeare and American history. For the most part, administrators have acquiesced to what they have perceived to be the demands of the marketplace. Although adaptive strategies may have secured the necessary funds for college survival, they have stripped liberal education of its central role and its meaning. Viewing students as markets or consumers encourages colleges to operate in a manner similar to for-profit businesses. In essence, consumer demands drive institutional operations as long as profits remain stable or rise.

College presidents and senior administrators have seen few alternatives. Aging physical facilities demand maintenance; few individuals gave thought to who would pay for the upkeep of the many buildings that were constructed in the 1960s. Even though faculty salaries have not kept pace with inflation, professors hired in the 1960s cost substantially more in the 1980s simply because of the disproportionate number of senior faculty. In large part because of a lack of perceived choice, administrators have turned to part-time or nontenured track faculty as way to reduce costs. The proportion of faculty who teach part-time has risen from 23 percent in 1966 to 41 percent in 1980.

Clearly, the teaching profession has suffered. Part-time faculty, by their very definition, cannot give as much time or attention to advising students as full-time faculty. The role of part-timers is to teach a class and not to become involved in student life. Part-time faculty also have little or no voice in the workings of the university, so that power and authority devolve into the hands of fewer individuals than previously. And, obviously, more part-time faculty implies fewer full-time faculty, which contributes to a scarcity of tenure-track jobs. The attractiveness of the profession also declines with diminished opportunity.

The proportion of entering college freshmen who intend to pursue careers as college professors has declined from 1.8 percent in 1966 to 0.2 percent in 1982—an 89 percent decline. Along with Russell Jacoby, many individuals today see the lives of college faculty as irrelevant to the concerns of society. In *The Last Intellectuals* Jacoby notes, "It is difficult for an educated adult American to name a single political scientist or sociologist or philosopher. . . . The professionals have abandoned the public arena" (1987, p. 190).

Jacoby and others feel that academic life no longer deals with the central issues of the United States. Instead, the professoriate has created private dialogues with itself. As opposed to enjoying the fruits of academic freedom, the faculty has reveled in "the freedom to be academic." Specialized courses and esoteric knowledge have divorced the university from society and the professoriate has become increasingly unable to provide a coherent argument for the mission of the university—the purpose of higher learning—and the role of the faculty in decision making.

In many respects, the manner in which recent critics have analyzed problems in higher education has made it difficult, if not impossible, for anyone to rebut the critics' arguments. Simply stated, once one has called for organizational effectiveness, or quality, or excellence, it becomes difficult, if not absurd, to provide a counterargument. Who can reasonably argue for ineffectiveness or mediocrity? If the argument has been phrased that we must make American higher education effective, then to raise rebuttals makes it appear as if one is against excellent, effective institutions. Since the parameters of the discourse have been set, it has been difficult to provide alternative ways of thinking about the nature of the collegiate curriculum.

The recent critics have not only dominated the discussion about the nature and purpose of higher education, they have also set the terms around which curricular solutions have been proposed. For example, curricular coherence has been advocated for what we conceive to be an educated person reared in Western society who must confront the technological imperatives of the twenty-first century. Educators have called for a reassertion of "leadership" on the part of collegiate presidents (Kerr & Gade, 1987) and higher admission standards and graduation requirements. Demonstrable improvements in student knowledge, capacities, and skills have also been demanded.

Most striking in the recent criticisms and solutions of higher education is the failure to join the issue of effectiveness and efficiency to the values of academic freedom and democracy. In other words, what the critics missed in their analyses is a democratic conception of college life, one that views administrators and faculty as more than transmitters of disembodied knowledge to a passive constituency. The critics have not considered how administrators and faculty might create an imaginative vision of citizenship for students so that they are empowered to critically assess and operate in the complex world of the twenty-first century. Instead, we have narrowed our focus to the vocational skills and historical facts of Western society that we perceive students will need for the future.

Admittedly, democracy is a difficult and confusing term to define. For the purpose of this book, democracy is conceived as those principles that promote social justice, equality, diversity, and empowerment. The enactment of democracy takes place by way of the manifold social formations and practices that occur in an organization. Speaking about democracy in this manner suggests that preparation for participating in a democracy is more than readjusting power relationships. Democracy concerns the most microscopic organizational activities that help constitute the nature of society, of the organization, and of knowledge.

Suggesting that we think about curricular formations in light of democracy advocates that we turn much of the logic of the previous decade about effectiveness and efficiency on its head. Rather than upholding the belief that organizational effectiveness and efficiency is a desired end in itself, the present work develops a view of organizational life that defines colleges and universities as cultures that are part of an ongoing movement and struggle for democracy. In doing so, it subscribes to the notion that college and university members are intellectuals who both introduce students to and legitimate a particular way of life.

Such a notion does not mean that we can concoct one best curricular model for all institutions, or that students will need specific skills during the rest of their lives. Instead, democratic participation is viewed as a way to summarize many of the skills students will need. In short, to speak for democracy is not to speak against effectiveness; democracy and effectiveness are not naturally contradictory notions. However, as will be shown, the theoretical notions of the effectiveness school are contradictory to the concept of an organization as socially constructed.

The view of democracy advocated here is pluralistic; in the system of higher education we have room for many different vistas. The imperative for the researcher is to view the organization in a manner so that we hear the multitude of organizational voices—not only the dominant, but also the silent; not only those who are powerful because of their position, such as presidents, but also those who lack positional power, such as students. The implications for this critical approach to the curriculum is that the silences of women or minorities, for example, in prevalent knowledge forms have to be noted to understand how knowledge has been constructed, who has constructed it, and what alternative constructions are possible. What follows is a discussion of the methodological tools used to locate the data.

RESEARCH DESIGN AND METHODOLOGY

Michael Apple notes, "The constant struggle to be clear is just that—a struggle. It is hard work to be understandable" (1986, p. 204). It is an equally hard struggle constantly to monitor oneself and check one's interpretations with the data at hand. A variety of writers are currently engaged in defining how to ensure one's data-trustworthiness in educational research that assumes an openly ideological stance (Smith, 1988; Lincoln, 1988; Lather, 1986).

The approach taken in this work follows a relatively new path in qualitative research tentatively called "critical ethnography." Although the basic tenets of critical ethnography have been widely employed in the field of anthropology, the approach is still relatively new in higher education. McLaughlin (1987), McLaren (1986), Willis (1977), and Weis (1985), among others, have followed the anthropological call for delineating the preconceived notions of the researcher as he or she describes those people under study. Critical ethnography rejects the idea that researchers can be value-neutral, and instead, strives to understand how concepts such as power and ideology constrain individuals. Critical ethnographers concur with Lather: "Scientific 'neutrality' and 'objectivity' serve to mystify the inherently ideological nature of research in the human sciences. . . . Research which is openly value based is neither more nor less ideological than is mainstream positivist research" (1986, p. 63). Ultimately, the goal of critical ethnography is not only to describe a particular group or organization, but also to promote social justice and empowerment of all people (Simon & Dippo, 1986).

The ethnographer has a multitude of choices when he or she wishes to investigate culture in an organization. Although preliminary attempts have been made at administering cultural surveys, most cultural researchers reject the value of data collection that cannot unearth the meaning of the responses. A deductive survey or questionnaire that seeks to decontextualize and synthesize data about curricula is anathema to the theoretical underpinnings of this work. The purpose here is not to test hypotheses or homogenize the cacophony of voices that construct a curriculum, but instead, to bring the polyphony to life. This project, then, followed Geertz's call for undertaking an "ethnography of modern thought." He states that such an ethnography will: "deepen even further our sense of the radical variousness of the way we think now" (1983, p. 161).

What was needed, then, was an approach that allowed for the different participants' voices to be heard. Essentially two choices existed: either to undertake an in-depth ethnography of one institution or conduct multiple case studies. Trade-offs exist for either approach. On the one hand, ethnography allows for the thickest of descriptions (Geertz, 1973) of the daily lives of the people under study. Case studies, on the other hand, provide for a fuller accounting of groupings of people, and the researcher is able to compare and contrast how people react to similar problems. Yet, ethnography lacks comparability, while case studies miss the richness of description that a year's study at one site affords.

The choice of case studies was made for a number of reasons. Having previously conducted a year-long ethnography (Tierney, 1988) and seven intensive case studies (Chaffee & Tierney, 1988) and to gain a fresh perspective and to remain open in my own ideological formulations, I followed a different methodological path with this study. Using a comparative study enabled widening my objective lens somewhat by standing clear of the nets of institutional power. Moreover, the research project was designed around seven case studies to extend an understanding of the concerns of different cadres of people—faculty, administrators, and students—to name three primary groups. As full a description as possible was developed—given the limitations of time and personpower—of the curricular discourses one hears on campuses.

The concern was not to validate the data, but rather to show the differences and similarities in constructions about the curriculum uncovered during site visits conducted throughout the academic year 1987–88. Instead of trying to validate and synthesize how one type of institution—public state colleges, for example—enacted their curriculum, a broad diversity of institutional types was sought. Five institutions were private, and two were public. Four were colleges and three were universities. The oldest institution was over 100 years old; the youngest was under 25. One institution was a women's institution, and another was Christian. The institutions were in urban and rural areas throughout the United States.

Over 250 people were interviewed, individually and in small and large groups. Curricular affairs meetings, executive committee meetings, and departmental meetings are included among the observations. From these interviews and meetings were collected a wealth of historical and documentary evidence about each institution and its curriculum.

The limitations to the endeavor are evident. Given the small sample size, two-year or proprietary institutions were not included. Since the interest was in providing analyses of concepts and roles, there is not the richness of data about individual institutions of my other work (Tierney, 1988; Chaffee & Tierney, 1988). However, the format of this book is unique for studies of curriculum in higher education. As the discussion in the preceding section has highlighted, this work was not undertaken simply to provide the reader with rationalist observations irrespective of a theoretical framework. In contrast, this study emphasizes the dialectical nature of society and theory by joining observation with critical reflection and understanding. As Giroux notes, "One begins not with an observation but with a theoretical framework that situates the observation in rules and conventions that give it meaning while simultaneously acknowledging the limitations of such a perspective" (1983, p. 20). Thus, this study seeks to bring a fresh perspective into our thinking about curricular matters in academe. The Appendix describes at greater length the approach utilized in the field to gather the data and the format used to ensure that the data was trustworthy. What follows is a brief guide to the text for the reader.

READING THE TEXT

Obviously, stories can be told in many ways. For example, one could tell the tale of Chaco Canyon chronologically, through the eyes of the original inhabitants, the Anasazi, or through the words of Ignacio Chavez and Joaquin Maesta, the first foreign visitors to the canyon in 1768. One might relate the events in the life of one individual or reveal the geological changes the canyon has undergone. Similarly, individual case studies could have been provided and the findings synthesized in a final chapter. Particular curricular innovations could have been highlighted and how they took place analyzed. I have chosen, instead, to delineate the discourses around specific concepts by particular actors.

Like a good mountain trail, a story that works must be well made, and a plethora of names and characters would only create confusion in a book intended to highlight the varieties of discourses that occur about the curriculum. Rather than tell seven individual stories of institutions, I have merged the institutional portraits to provide a fuller range of the language that takes place over the contested terrain of curricular matters. We hear people speak about their lives and their institutions as if we are there when they are speaking their lines.

The next chapter offers an overview of organizational culture which will provide the reader with an understanding of what to look for in subsequent chapters. Organizational culture is considered as an ideological frame that provides participants with a sense of meaning and direction about the nature of the organization and higher education.

Throughout Part II we hear the words of the people interviewed and observed—students, faculty, administrators, parents, community representatives, and trustee members. Their words are related to the concept of what an institution says it is—its mission—and we see how what the organizational participants say they are gets played out in the curriculum.

Part III discusses faculty and administrators because they ostensibly play a crucial role in defining and shaping the curriculum. In the world of higher education it is commonplace to assign academic leadership, managerial responsibilities, and decision-making authority to faculty and academic administrators. Through the words of the multiple constituencies we will hear various perceptions of faculty and administrators on their role in academic leadership.

It should be pointed out that faculty and administrators are linked together not because they have similar viewpoints, but because we need to consider more closely the relationship of the two. As will become clearer in the subsequent chapter, I do not subscribe to the notion that one group—administrators, in this case—consciously holds power and wields it as a weapon. Administrators, as much as faculty or students or the community, are entangled in the ideological terrain of culture. Not until we understand the dynamics at work with all groups will we be able to forge successful strategies of empowerment. As will be shown, the curriculum often becomes contested landscape of the social constructions faculty and administrators develop about one another and toward the curriculum.

To reiterate, as the book unfolds, three topics will be considered: (1) how actors support or bring into question the school's mission and thus socially construct the curriculum as part of a cultural process; (2) how the curriculum can more forcefully serve as a democratic change agent that empowers; and (3) what strategies faculty and administrators might consider to further the empowerment process.

Pierre Bourdieu observes that it is often necessary to reconstitute "the complexity of the social world in a language capable of holding together the most diverse things while setting them in rigorous perspective. It prevents the reader from slipping back into . . . simplicities" (quoted in Apple, 1986, p. 202). The expectation for this work is that it will show "the complexity of the social world," but it is also hoped to portray those complexities in clear language. The reader comes into contact with those interviewed and observed by way of the text. Out of these mutual discourses we will move toward understanding how we might enable the curriculum to enlighten and empower.

2

Interpreting the Terrain

This chapter offers the reader the conceptual tools for interpreting the activities that take place in the subsequent chapters. Just as archaeologists need to prepare themselves for an excavation, developing an understanding of organizational culture will give the reader a sense of what to look for in the seven institutions. The preceding chapter outlined the landscape of the curriculum in higher education; this chapter sets the reader on the road to interpreting that landscape. It divides into three parts: First, it outlines the functional approach to culture, and then explicates the critical approach. The shortcomings of the functionalist approach are critiqued, and the critical approach to culture is offered as an alternative to use in discussing the curriculum. The reader then is offered a map of the terrain for Parts II and III.

How writers use the idea of culture relates directly to the epistemological foundations on which they base their analysis. Our view of organizational reality is determined by initial questions and assumptions and the nature of the investigation, the methodology, and the research findings vary accordingly. To illustrate the differences between a functional and a critical approach to culture, then, the underlying assumptions, purposes, and manifestations of each perspective are outlined.

The decision to discuss functional and critical approaches to culture is purposeful. Fundamental differences exist between the two approaches. As will become clear, the functional approach to organizational culture is the predominant one. A critical study of culture bases itself on entirely different premises. As opposed to goals of effectiveness and e:ficiency, the concepts of democracy and empowerment receive primary attention.

As we consider the functional and critical approaches to organizational culture in higher education, four questions will guide the investigation. First, what is an educational institution's relationship to society? Second, how does an institution define, translate, and experience its mission? Third, by what methods do researchers guide their inquiry? Fourth, what are the implications of the cultural approach for the study of the curriculum?

THE FUNCTIONAL APPROACH TO CULTURE

The cultural functionalist premise about the nature of higher education is that colleges and universities are institutions that socialize the young to societal mores and truths. Higher education serves the needs of society. In this light, the underlying function of a college or university is to include common values, skills, and knowledge.

If the institutional mandate is to reflect the greater society, then the study of culture in an educational organization assumes that organizations are not change agents; organizations mirror and reproduce reality. The goal for analysis is to comprehend cultural aspects of the organization so that cultural elements will function effectively in reproducing reality. Masland, for example, has commented on the need to study organizational culture in colleges and universities: "Analysis of culture may expose conflicting cultural elements which could lead to ineffective behavior and plans" (1985, p. 166).

Culture, loosely defined by functionalists as shared values and beliefs, has three key functions. First, culture provides organizational members with a sense of meaning and identity. Second, culture shapes behavior; participants act in one way and not another because of the parameters of the culture. Third, strong cultures increase organizational stability and effectiveness.

The basic assumptions of cultural functionalists about the nature of organizational reality are similar to the tenets of bureaucratic rationalism. One assumption is that the organization exists in a "real" world that is comprehensible both to the participants and to the researcher trying to understand the organization. The organizational world is comprised of objective, palpable structures that exist irrespective of human consciousness. In essence, the organizational world is understandable and finite. The organization equals the sum of its parts, and culture is one of those parts.

A further idea is that a normative, informal organizational structure exists that demands understanding and analysis. As with other organizational components, such as the social structure and the environment, culture exists as an interrelated variable in the organization. Culture influences components such as social structure, technology, and the environment, and those variables also influence organizational culture. Cultural components are manipulable and manageable by organizational participants. As a variable in the organization, managers utilize culture to increase effectiveness. When administrators orchestrate important ceremonies and rituals, for example, the assumption is that they are shaping the cultural dimensions of the organization.

Cultural dimensions derive from group experience and are learned behaviors. Consequently, one finds culture only where a definable group exists with a significant history. If an organization has a set of basic assumptions and beliefs and has shared a number of critical events over time, then the researcher can say that the organization has a culture. Conversely, groups without a history or shared beliefs lack culture. Schein states this point succinctly: "The organization as a whole may be found to have an overall culture if that whole organization has a significant shared history, but we cannot assume the existence of such a culture ahead of time" (1985, p. 8). From this perspective a distinctive college with a history, such as Reed or Swarthmore, can be said to have a culture, whereas a new, urban commuter community college will probably lack a culture.

Assumptions about culture abound, including the notions that strong cultures are more effective than weak cultures (Deal & Kennedy, 1982) or particular management practices foster culture more effectively than others (Peters & Waterman, 1982). They exemplify the belief on the part of functionalists that culture can be counted; culture equals objects, acts, and events. Organizational participants produce culture. Various components of culture, such as ceremonies, rites, and traditions (Pfeffer, 1981; Trice & Beyer, 1984), organizational stories (Hirsch & Andrews, 1983), and symbolism (March, 1984; Gudykunst, 1985) have been investigated to understand the structure and function of organizational culture in order to teach administrators how to be more effective in their cultural management.

In sum, culture is a causal variable that makes organizations more effective. Culture changes and can be changed by a variety of devices. For example, Peters and Waterman (1982) have offered "management by walking around" as a tool that has an explicitly cultural function. Good cultural managers walk around their buildings and get to know their employees; bad ones sit in their offices. Good managers communicate orally; bad ones write impersonal memos. Good managers have an open-door policy, symbolizing collegiality; poor ones exhibit little concern for subordinates' feelings or opinions. Thus, the job of the manager is to use cultural tools to achieve concrete, specific organizational goals.

Managers have times when they ought to act culturally; functionalists also believe that times exist when managers do not act culturally. As an organizational variable, culture is not pervasive; managers sometimes act in the absence of culture. Similarly, certain objects are imbued with cultural value and other objects are void of cultural worth. A president's speech at graduation, or the act of graduation itself, can be a cultural act. The building of a budget or long-range plan, however, might not be viewed as cultural. The goal for the manager is not only to comprehend the organization's culture, but also to understand the appropriate times to act culturally.

Thus, the functionalist premise is that four basic assumptions shape the nature of organizational culture and reality. First, functionalists assume that culture is cognitive and can be understood by participants and researchers. Second, they assume that a culture that functions effectively has manifest meaning; all participants interpret cultural artifacts similarly. Third, they assume that it is possible to codify abstract realities. Fourth, the researcher assumes that culture can be predictable and generalizable. In a functional world, the assumption is that objective events such as rituals or ceremonies are predictors of objective circumstances such as productivity, and subjective perceptions such as commitment and satisfaction (Sypher, Applegate, & Sypher, 1985).

Through observation, researchers try to develop taxonomic schemas of the culture of the organization. Appropriating much of the terminology and framework of the American structural-functionalist school of the 1940s, functionalist researchers of organizational culture have struggled to uncover the functions of organizational components such

as rituals, ceremonies, or symbols. The assumption is that an understanding of how a cultural component such as a ritual function will aid
managers in their work.

Insofar as similar cultural artifacts exist from organization to organization, generalizability beyond the specific organizational setting is
possible. The implications for researchers are self-evident from the
theoretical assumptions. Researchers must look beyond structural for-
malities and toward symbolic behavior that nevertheless can be observed
and understood. Essentially nomothetic in nature, the methodological
endeavor is to uncover the abstract and universal laws of the organization. The researcher believes that systematic observation and interviews will uncover the culture of the organization.

The implications for the curriculum of a functional approach to culture
have been alluded to in the previous chapter. The assumption is that
the researcher operates from a morally neutral position. Since culture
is understandable to everyone, the impetus for the researcher is to
provide avenues for improving the fit between what an institution says
it is (its mission) with what it actually does (the curriculum). Even
though the mission is an abstraction, the assumption is that organizational leaders can codify the abstraction so that all people will have
similar interpretations. Since different organizations will perceive of
knowledge and their relationship to society similarly, the development
of a taxonomy of curricular models is desirable and possible.

The functional perspective maintains that empirical questions about
an institution's curriculum have answers that have little to do with
institutional or societal values and ideologies. In other words, cultural
functionalism refers to the extent to which a series of curricular actions
is organized in such a manner as leads to predetermined goals with
maximum efficiency. Cultural functionalism concerns the implemen-
tation of curricular goals, and not the selection of the goals. From this
perspective, to argue for an effective curriculum is merely to uphold
the essential goals of the organization.

THE CRITICAL APPROACH TO CULTURE

A critical view of educational organizations provides a quite different
picture of culture. Henry Giroux is worth quoting on defining critical
theory and the role it takes with regard to its purpose:

Critical theory [is] tied to a specific interest in the development of a society without injustice. Theory, in this case, becomes a transformative activity that views itself as explicitly political and commits itself to the projection of a future that is as yet unfulfilled. . . . Rather than proclaiming a [functionalist] notion of neutrality, critical theory openly takes sides in the interest of struggling for a better world (1983, p. 19).

Critical theorists eschew the morally neutral tone that functionalism or cultural functionalism seeks. They do not study an organization to learn whether or not a curriculum is effective and efficient without regard to its values. To critical theorists, the processes and goals of an organization are of central importance. Critical theorists envision college and university campuses that stand for freedom of inquiry and support the unhindered assertion, discussion, and development of ideas. Seen in this light, the curricular challenge for American postsecondary institutions is to embody an educational vision that is both enriched and tempered by the multicultural vitality of its people. From this perspective, educators need to develop curricular strategies that do not ultimately favor the economic and political interests of ruling groups, but give voice to the alienated and dominated.

To envision postsecondary education in this manner does not imply a myopic view of the world. The purpose of education is not to indoctrinate students to a singular worldview so that when they leave their institutions they are in lockstep with one another's ideas about the way the world works. Instead, higher education provides students with the capability to decide for themselves which avenues to take in the world. The failure of higher education to provide that forum for learning returns us to a discussion of efficiency and effectiveness.

The concept of educational organizations as a forum for developing critical thinking does not premise itself on quantitative measures of organizational effectiveness and efficiency but rather by way of democratic intent. Rather than assume that an organization exists as a reified rational object that is a construct of the larger society, critical theorists perceive the organization as a social construction of society and the participants within the organization. Based in a dialectical interplay between college community and society, the organization's purpose acts not just as a reflector of societal mores, but also as a democratic change agent that has transformational possibilities. Thus, a critical investigation of culture is incompatible with a view of an organization as a functional mechanism. An understanding of the culture of an organization will neither be derived from the assumption that culture is yet another tool to fix an ineffective machine, nor will culture be understood as an abstract or neutral term.

Critical theory's overarching premise is that the organization's culture focuses the participants' understanding of their relationship to society through an organizational web of patterns and meanings. Interpretation, interaction, and contestation are highlighted. Research focuses on the relationship of the organization's culture to the greater society, the determinacy of the contexts that surround and constitute the culture of the organization, and the role of the individual in constructing meaning. Such points are especially important when we consider the culture of an educational organization insofar as the purpose of education is tightly linked to the purposes of society.

The assumptions of a critical perspective of organizational culture are fourfold and stand in sharp distinction to rationalist premises. First, culture is not necessarily understandable either to organizational participants or researchers. Since culture is an act of interpretation, what each person observes and interprets varies. A second, related assumption is that organizational actions are mediated by equifinal processes. That is, the construction of meaning does not imply that all individuals interpret reality similarly. Third, it is impossible to codify abstract reality. Fourth, culture is interpretive, a dialectical process of negotiation between the researcher and the researched.

Culture is seen as a power-laden concept, not as a tool for increasing effectiveness. It acts to mediate the demands of the greater society with the struggles and perceptions of participants in the collegiate institutions. As opposed to the cultural functionalist, the critical theorist does not believe that culture is something that a manager can turn on or off; all action exists within a cultural web. "Management by walking around" or other functional notions stand in sharp contrast to the critical view of culture.

I am arguing for an approach to culture that assumes postsecondary institutions can neither be shielded from external interference and studied in a scientifically controlled environment, nor does the organization exist as a reified object. The social scientist's ability to comprehend events and the manager's ability to act are based in cultural definitions.

All social science and administrative action exists in a cultural world, amidst, to quote Clifford Geertz's well-worn phrase, "a web of significations we ourselves have spun" (1973, p. 5).

This approach begins with the assumption that the culture of an organization constitutes human existence to such an extent that both prediction and the ability to reduce organizational meaning to predetermined elements are impossible. Intentionality depends upon the culture's prior histories within which individuals constitute meaning for themselves. Rather than view reality as objective and external to the participants, the critical perspective assumes that reality is defined through a process of social interchange that cannot be readily mapped, graphed, or controlled. There is not one single, simple, unilinear rationality; there are many rationalities, depending on the mores of the enterprise, the individuals involved in the organization, and the sociohistorical context in which the organization resides.

Pierre Bourdieu's concept of the *habitus* is helpful in conceptualizing how to think of the relationship between history and the organization. Bourdieu defines habitus as "a system of lasting, transposable dispositions which, integrating past experiences, functions at every moment as a matrix of perceptions, appreciations and actions" (1977, p. 82). We may also think of the habitus as "a subjective but not individual system of internalized structures, schemes of perception, conception, and action common to all members of the same group or class" (1977, p. 86). To explain this concept a bit more simply, Bourdieu sees the habitus as a mixture of the attitudes, beliefs, and experiences of organizational participants.

The habitus interacts with objective history "which has accumulated over the passage of time in things, machines, buildings, monuments, books, theories, customs, laws, etc." (1981, p. 305), but it is not an objectified structure that participants passively accept. Critical theorists work from the assumption that history is an interaction between participants' lived, internalized experiences, and the ideological momentum that becomes institutionalized over the passage of time. The challenge is to understand how the interactions operate, how ideology becomes accepted, and how organizational participants create and are created by aspects of their culture.

Culture is not simply a decontextualized taxonomy of functional artifacts such as rituals and ceremonies. Instead, we locate culture in terms of its historical relationship to ideology and power. Giroux notes that culture "is a complex of traditions, institutions, and formations situated within a social sphere of contestation and struggle, a sphere rooted in a complex of power relations that influence and condition lived experiences without dictating their results" (1983, p. 164). Culture, then, both limits and enables human action. Organizational participants are both subjects and objects capable of inducing change while at the same time being constrained and guided by powerful ideological formations. In this light, society is a selector and filter of human action.

The suppositions of critical theory necessitate different investigations from those of the functionalist. Words such as ideology, power, authority, and empowerment receive attention instead of effectiveness and efficiency (McLaughlin, 1987). Cultural studies of educational organizations in general, and curricular matters in particular, do not focus on how the organization replicates society, but on the Deweyan idea of how educational organizations may help challenge the social order to develop and advance democracy.

The value of this approach is that it refuses to remain mired in modes of analysis that examine collegiate life from the singular perspective of effectiveness and efficiency. Theory acts in a dialectical nature with policy and practice. We no longer assume that a finite number of curricular models will define knowledge. Critical theorists strive to highlight how theoretical frameworks mediate between organizational participants and the larger social reality, thereby producing knowledge. Theory acts as a filter through which we define problems and reach answers so that we come to terms with the internal logics of different cultures.

Critical theory moves us beyond reproductive theories that seek to demonstrate how educational institutions only duplicate the social order. Culture is now investigated not merely as a simple tool of effectiveness, but rather as a cacophony of multivocal voices mediated within different layers of reality shaped by an interaction of dominant and subordinate forms of power. We observe not only the constraints placed on the human will, but also the possibilities for action and change. At the core of the critical approach is the recognition that power, knowledge, ideology, and culture are inextricably linked to one another in constantly changing patterns and relationships.

I define power in much the same light as Foucault when he says: "Power is everywhere: not because it embraces everything, but because it comes from everywhere. . . . Power is not an institution, nor a structure, nor a possession. It is the name we give to a complex strategic situation in a particular society'' (1978, p. 93).

In this light, as many forms of power exist as there are types of relationships. All groups and individuals within an organization exercise and are subjected to mechanisms of power. Certain categories of people—students, for example—have little ability to exercise power, but nevertheless, few members of groups fail to find some means of exercising power if only on one another (Tierney, 1988). For example, it is conceivable that students who drop out of school or perform poorly in school are demonstrating acts of resistance and a negative exercise of power.

Power, then, is not another administrative tool merely to be used by politically minded managers. No one can escape the web of power; we are all enmeshed in it. The most debilitating aspect of power is when we, as organizational participants, have internalized accepted forms of authority to such an extent that we are unable to envision ourselves as anything other than passive recipients of dominant norms. Our challenge is to consider strategies that enable organizational actors to understand the contours by which they are constrained and develop ways to empower those who are subjugated by dominating influences.

To speak of empowerment means more than enabling the powerless to assume powerful positions in the organization. Although it is important to be concerned with enabling underrepresented groups to assume perceived positions of power such as college presidencies, we cannot be content with only that goal. For example, for women and people of color to assume executive positions in colleges and universities is crucial; but the elevation of one group is not enough if the organizational relations of power remain the same. We need to develop empowering strategies that go beyond struggles for individual achievement. We must develop strategies of empowerment whereby organizational participants are able to think and act critically. Giroux and McLaren observe that this form of empowerment concerns the ability of participants ''to interrogate and selectively appropriate those aspects of the dominant culture that will provide them with the basis for defining and transforming, rather than merely serving, the wider social order'' (1986, p. 229).

As power represents configurations of force, mainstream ideology represents the implicit discourse of the dominant. By ideology, I mean ''the set of basic beliefs, or set of practices, which in some ways helps to constitute or shape individual consciousness and which orients humans in the world and guides belief and action'' (Siegel, 1987, p. 154). Geertz has noted that ideologies are essentially symbolic systems that make "otherwise incomprehensible situations meaningful" (1973, p. 220). In other words, the concept of ideology concerns the taken for granted assumptions participants have about the organization. Ideology defines the parameters of discourse that will occur in the organization so that participants come to make sense of their own experiences. As the concept is used in this book, ideology will refer not only to a specific doctrine, but also will be investigated in light of how the cultures of colleges and universities sustain and produce ideologies. The investigation will examine how ideology exists through the systematization of spatial, temporal, and symbolic arrangements in the organization. Also to be examined are how individuals and groups come to negotiate, resist, or accept the dominant ideologies of their organizations. An analysis of this kind necessitates unearthing the manner in which domination is concealed at the institutional level and throughout the system.

It should be clear why the study of ritual events, such as highly significant ceremonies, will not in and of themselves be helpful for comprehending the organizational universe. Similarly, studies that lack an understanding of the specific actions of an organization will also misinterpret how organizational ideologies operate. To understand culture, power, and ideology we must see not only the grand actions of an organization, such as an overtly symbolic presidential speech, but we must also see the contextual circumstances that surround the speech; we must understand the microscopic activities that make up the cultural life of the organization through which the participants experience ideology. We will see not only how ideologies are imposed on participants, but also how people both openly resist and silently conform.

From this perspective, culture, power, and ideology are closely intertwined. Culture here is viewed as the arena wherein ideology and power are enacted. It is more than the sum of symbolic objects that have been observed in an organization. Culture is the terrain where dominant ideologies and mechanisms of power come together to reproduce and create a specific kind of society. The researcher's task is to comprehend how those reproductions and creations occur.

MAPPING THE TERRAIN

The landscape to be portrayed is difficult to envisage. Most literature on the curriculum covers familiar territory and, as readers, we know how to respond. For example, because we usually assume that knowledge is a concrete entity, it is relatively easy for us to enter into a discussion about whether we want our sons and daughters to read more Chaucer and less Kerouac or vice versa. Because we live and work in higher education organizations, we have little difficulty in commenting on whether or not our college presidents should speak out more forcefully on curricular matters. Such issues may provide different answers from time to time, but the terrain remains the same.

I propose that we embark on a different journey. We will look at the culture of seven institutions through the words of the organizational participants. Following the definitions provided in Part I, we will investigate the complex of contradictory voices that characterize an organization's culture, and the power of individuals and organizations to define and legitimate particular views of reality, and the ideological apparatus of the culture. The reader will hear not only the dominant participants' views of reality; but will also see the interstices of the organization so that the silences that take place will become evident. Accordingly, knowledge is viewed as neither neutral nor objective; instead, the curriculum is viewed as a social construction that embodies specific interests and assumptions. By linking knowledge and the curriculum with the concepts of power and ideology we will search for the manner in which the organization aids the participants in understanding the processes in which they are situated.

Part II opens with the explanations the participants give to the two most familiar words educators use when they discuss academic affairs— *mission* and *curriculum*. Hearing the dissonance uncovered not only across institutions, but also within the institutions as well, what are we to make of the multiplicity of interpretations the participants provide?

Part III focuses more closely on the voices of the principle participants—faculty and administrators. We hear not only their voices, but we also listen to how others view the faculty and administrators. It will appear odd at times, if not impossible, that some of these individuals are traversing the same trail at the same time. Is it possible to orchestrate the organization in a less cacophonous manner?

II
Words

Let [the student] be asked for an account not merely of the words of his lesson, but of its sense and substance and let him judge the profits he has made by the testimony not of his memory, but of his life. Let him be made to show what he has just learned in a hundred aspects, and apply it to as many different subjects, to see if he has yet properly grasped it and made it his own.

Michel Eyquem de Montaigne

3

Cartographies: The Institutional Mission

At Testimony State College, an institution with a liberal tradition, a faculty member of seven years reflects:

It has taken a long time to understand what this place is about, the mission of this place. I like going different places. This is the fifth college I've taught at, and it is the most difficult to understand. I remember a party one time and it was almost a series of testimonials. One after another a faculty member got up and said "What this place meant to me." I was aghast! It was very, very discomfiting. For everybody else it was routine. They had seen the light, the truth, and I was just one of the novitiates.

At Cutting Edge College, which offers interdisciplinary coursework, an individual comments, "The mission gets mystified here. Sometimes people embrace it with a religious fervor and I wonder. We think we're special. Everyone is special, different." At a third institution, Working Class State College, a new faculty member adds, "I was at a conservative Christian college before coming here. I don't see much of a difference between there and here. I'd say our mission at both places is to teach. Same kind of students. Same mission."

What makes these comments interesting is not only the diversity of views the three faculty members take of their institutions, but also how

easy it is for them to speak about "what this place is about." One
individual is amazed how his liberal public state college can be so
insular, and another person reflects outwardly about how every institution is unique. A third individual sees little difference between a
religious college and a public college. Each of these comments highlights the essential point of this chapter: People need to make sense of
their organizational lives; and if the institutional mission is unclear,
they will make it clear for themselves.

I discuss the mission of an institution from a variety of perspectives.
The first part considers what an institutional mission is by discussing
how it gets defined and interpreted. The second section explores how
people learn about a mission by looking at who defines the mission.
Finally, we reflect on how people know if their institution is doing what
the mission prescribes.

"DEFINING OUR LIVES"

When queried about the mission of Classics College a student comments on his institution by saying, "It's supposed to define our lives.
You know, tell us what we're about. The word about this place is
'intense.' It's about intense learning."

Often, when asked about their institution's mission, people define it
in a manner similar to the above student. Participants define the mission
of the institution as if the organizational identity is holographic. People
interpret the organization as a unity as opposed to a more ideographic
form where separate organizational units are cognizant that an institutional mission exists, but the identity of the subunit is where one gains
understanding and meaning (Albert & Whetten, 1985).

An example of an ideographic form is *Entrepreneurial College* (EC).
Entrepreneurial College is an institution with a wealthy, articulate student body, a faculty with a strong reputation, and a beautiful campus
facility. Full-time faculty are about 250, and student FTE enrollment
is close to 3,500. Tuition is over $10,000. Entrepreneurial is close to
150 years old. Over 80 percent of the freshman class will graduate
within four years. The top administration has undergone changes during
the last few years due in part to retirements and acceptance of jobs
elsewhere. In some respects the previous administration had been seen
as superfluous; however, the present president, academic vice president,

and school deans seem to have formed a team that is slowly gaining begrudging respect from the faculty and student body.

Entrepreneurial College is an institution that operates in what one individual terms "the entrepreneurial model." "No, we really don't know what we're about other than what everyone else is about—teaching, research, service. What we are, what's great, is that people can go out and start something if they want to. It's like starting a small business." In another interview at Entrepreneurial College a senior professor agrees: "There's lots of flexibility here. There are lots of spaces to do things so we can scoot through the cracks. It's like the ad they use for the Army. 'Be all you can be!' " An ideographic form, then, is where little, if any, consensus exists about the mission other than in the most general terms.

A holographic institution is one where a seemingly tight identity governs all actions of the institution. *Christian University* (CU) is a good example of such an institution. Christian is close to 100 years old. For a private institution, tuition is relatively low at around $6,000. Faculty size is close to 200, and the student body is at 3,000. In many respects Christian University is a college "on the move." The small urban campus is about to undergo several renovation projects. The fiscal base of the college appears to be growing, although many people are unhappy that a capital campaign has not gotten under way. People are confident that Christian University could meet the goals set by a fundraising campaign. The student body has expanded from a local to a regional clientele. The business and educational community in which Christian University is located looks favorably on the institution and a strong continuing education component has been added. The president is devoutly religious and often preaches on campus or in churches throughout the town and region. The vast majority of faculty, staff, and administrators are Christian who profess to work at the college because of its mission. A student comments:

Being a Christian in a public high school was tough. People made fun of me. I very much wanted a college that was dedicated to a Christian way of life. People acknowledge God here, so I don't have to defend myself. It's allowed me to find the truth, rather than push me into the corner.

Consistently, throughout the institution people speak of Christianity as the central focus for what they do. The president refers to the mission as "a living document." A philosophy professor notes, "The university's first commitment is to truth within a broadly Christian framework. Everything we do must be devoted to that."

Previous research has often distinguished between ideographic and holographic when discussing the mission of higher education. Most often, people have spoken for a holographic identity to forestall organizational confusion. Zammuto, reflecting others (Mortimer & Tierney, 1979; Chaffee, 1984; Peck, 1984; Keller, 1983) has commented: "A clear understanding of and consensus about mission is essential for an institution to successfully cope with a period of decline" (1986, p. 53). These writers argue that a clear mission is critical as a measuring stick to assess the appropriateness of individualized programs.

Other writers have gone so far as to claim that institutions have "lost their way" because they have deviated from their historic mission. In speaking about land-grant universities, for example, Schuh bemoans the loss of institutional commitment to public service and applied research. He states, "Presidents, deans, and faculty must reinstill a mission orientation into our land-grant universities. They must revitalize the tripartite mission of teaching, research and extension" (1986, p. 7).

On the other hand, Davies speaks for a more ideographic form of institution: "It is in no one's interest that missions be defined clearly. Institutions do not appear to engage in rigorous definition of their missions because the prevailing incentives are to do otherwise" (1986, p. 88). Chait echoes Davies by saying, "The more one seeks specificity, the more various constituencies resist. In the end, vague and vapid goals able to attract consensus are preferable to precise aims that force choices and provoke serious disagreements" (1979, p. 36).

Given the disagreement about whether an institution should try to specify its mission statement, we return to *Cutting Edge College* (CEC) where the faculty member spoke of the "religious fervor" that the institution holds for some. At $12,000, Cutting Edge has the highest tuition of any of the seven institutions under study. Student enrollment is a little over 1,000, and faculty size hovers around 90. About 60 percent of the student body graduates within four years. Cutting Edge sits in an idyllic setting in a semirural environment. Although the physical plant is not so luxurious as that of Entrepreneurial College, the campus is primarily functional rather than run-down or dilapidated.

The president and academic vice president work closely together as a team, and they appear to have earned the widespread respect and admiration of the faculty. Because Cutting Edge is a young institution, barely over 20 years old, they have been unable to rely on alumni contributions. Their financial base is shaky, but not in danger of collapse. The student body is bright and articulate and drawn from throughout the country. Cutting Edge has a deserved reputation as being "left-of-center" so that the student body is quite different than at either Christian University or Entrepreneurial College. Similarly, the faculty is a hardworking group of primarily liberal intellectuals who value teaching over research, although by no means is there consensus about what the balance between teaching and research should be.

One faculty member who has been at the college for over 15 years ruminates about the mission and succinctly states:

I'm not sure what it is. There's a rich mix of what we emanate. We're a teaching college, but some of us also think research is important. Some don't. We have a reputation for being artsy-folksy. The faculty have an unstated goal to social change. Admissions information is contractual-formal, it focuses on jobs, how we make people think. We also have an interdisciplinary focus that is student centered. So you tell me, what's our mission?

Cutting Edge College in some respects can be said to be both ideographic and holographic. The new faculty member, mentioned at the outset of this chapter, sees the institution in terms of an overarching ideology that defines the institution as tightly as a religion. The professor mentioned above sees more of a diffusion of purpose; the college is one concept to one constituency and another concept to another constituency.

Another senior faculty member at Cutting Edge defines the mission yet again differently. She states, "It's important to us that we're on the cutting edge. That's how I'd define it. We're dedicated to teaching ideas, not facts. And those ideas are on the cutting edge. We've done that since day one, and I'd say we'll still be doing it ten years from now." Another individual agrees with the idea of defining the mission in terms of being on the "cutting edge," but plays up how the mission gets defined. "The students always tell us we're selling out. It's strange that they're the ones who are the most adamant about us keeping our mission." A student concurs, "We [students] know what this place stands for. It's for inquiry. Knowledge. Self-learning. They try to make it appear normal so they won't have to worry about dollars, so they can attract more students here.''

The point about this mixed group of responses is that how participants define and interpret an organizational mission is inevitably contradictory. In part organizational participants define the institutional mission with regard to the constituency they wish to reach. The constituency may or may not define the mission in the intended manner. Other constituencies also exist that will make sense of the mission from their own orientations.

A cultural view of organizational mission concerns itself more with the symbolic manifestations of a mission than the assumption that institutions are *either* ideographic *or* holographic. The mission of an institution is a cultural production based on competing perceptions of organizational reality. At Cutting Edge, Christian University, and Entrepreneurial College, the interpretation of the mission is an ideological process through which the various participants experience themselves, their relations to others, and the institution's relationship in society.

Inevitably, differing interpretations take place. At Christian University, for example, the student commented that he attended the institution because the basic teachings of the institution reinforced his beliefs. At Cutting Edge College, faculty and students constantly challenge, reinforce, and reinterpret one another's perception of the institution's mission. Entrepreneurial College allows participants considerable leeway to ''scoot through the cracks.'' From this perspective, the organizational mission concerns more than a managerial strategy for creating an effective organization of one kind of another; the mission of an organization also concerns how institutional ideology operates through the manipulation of symbols to construct a particular identity that constituencies then interpret.

An institution's ideology is not something that simply gets created in the mind of the organizational leader or administrators and then gets imposed throughout the organization. Instead, as Newton and Rosenfelt put it, ideology is a ''system of representations (discourse, images, myths) through which we experience ourselves in relation to each other and to the social structures in which we live'' (quoted in Giroux, 1987, p. 115). And by ''experiencing ourselves'' we interpret the institution by way of our own previous experiences at other colleges, other universities.

What ''discourses, images, myths'' of organizations lead to the creation of an ideology? Individuals may attach significance to any number of phenomena, yet it is in the context of the organization that symbols acquire shared meaning. A key to understanding organizational symbols is to delineate the symbolic forms whereby the participants communicate, perpetuate, and develop their knowledge about and attitudes toward life (Tierney, 1989). How do symbols acquire shared meaning? Who plays a role in the creation of the symbols and ideology? Who manipulates the symbols, and who interprets them? By turning to a consideration of how people learn the mission of their institution and which actors play a role in defining the mission for them, we will analyze these questions.

DEFINING AND INTERPRETING

Between my visits to the campus of Entrepreneurial College in the fall and spring three faculty members are denied tenure. The rumor is that the individuals have not published enough. The reverberations echo throughout the campus. The tenure denials are a major topic of conversation among senior faculty. Students sign petitions. Junior faculty silently worry what the denials mean for *their* chances to gain tenure. At lunch one day with three junior faculty, the following conversation ensues:

Faculty # 1: I don't stand in the hallways now and talk with students. I don't like it because teaching isn't important.

Faculty # 2: Everyone scurries into their office now. It's scary. Maybe I'm not hearing things right. You can't find an assistant professor now, because we're all trying to get our articles out.

Faculty # 3. I think we're two-faced. We talk about teaching. The search committee tells you how important teaching is, and as soon as you get here, the terms change. It's not fair. It's a misrepresentation.

Faculty # 2: And it doesn't help that two of them were women who were active in women's studies either. I'm interested in interdisciplinary studies, but now I wouldn't touch it, won't get near it.

Faculty # 1: It's the administration's doing. The president is a manager, an enforcer of trustee ideas.

Faculty # 2: I think it's from the deans and provost. They're trying to make this a fancier place.

Faculty # 1: It seems like we're spinning our wheels, wasting our time, when we should be talking about the curriculum. Isn't that what a teaching institution is about?

Faculty # 3: I don't know if I can physically stand it.

Faculty # 1: I spend a lot of time on grant proposals.

Faculty # 3: I really enjoyed talking and interacting with students. . . .

Faculty # 1: I want everything "to count" now. Pass the sugar, would you?

Ostensibly, three faculty in different disciplines and schools have interpreted the mission similarly. In a later discussion they all relate that when they left graduate school they had wanted to find a faculty job that focused on teaching; they wanted to continue doing research, and they did not want to work in a "publish or perish" institution. The search committee at Entrepreneurial College had reaffirmed each of their hopes; the candidates had interpreted from their campus visits that the institution was a teaching institution. Given the tenure denials, however, their assumptions about the mission are shaken.

Yet, in conversations with the president, academic vice president, one school dean, and the chair of the tenure review committee at EC, all comment that they feel no criteria for tenure have changed. The faculty member who chairs the tenure review committee comments:

This institution prides itself on allowing its faculty to choose, within some limits, its contribution to the school. Are they excellent in the avenues they have chosen? But no amount of strength in one area can overcome a radical deficiency in another area. I've been here twenty years. We did not single these three people out or change our criteria this year.

Each of the individuals who speaks with me and who has reviewed the files of the three denials has reached the same conclusion. The individuals have published almost nothing and consequently should not be granted tenure.

The issue is not whether a mistake was made about granting someone tenure. The example also goes beyond accounting for whether teaching is more important than research. The tenure denials and the junior faculty's interpretation of them stand as a vivid illustration of how people learn about and redefine their institutional mission. The event is a multitude of lessons to junior faculty, not only about the reward structure, but also about what it means to be a faculty member. In essence, they have learned about the difference between academic appearance and organizational reality.

One event such as a tenure denial is not enough to bring the mission of Entrepreneurial College into question if every other symbolic expression is uniformly consistent about the nature of teaching and faculty life. However, as noted above, the mission of EC does not narrowly define what someone can or cannot do. Instead, broad definitions exist; individuals operate within the contexts of the definitions and provide their own interpretations. When clear examples arise, such as a denial of tenure, the individual reformulates an understanding of the institution. Curiously, the redefinition does not so much promote what the institution *is*, but what it is *not*. It is not that the institution is for research, but that it does not reward teaching.

The next example is a quite different instance of how people learn about and interpret the mission of their institution. This institution, referred to earlier as one where faculty gave "testimony" to its value in their lives, is a relatively new, relatively liberal, public institution. As opposed to Entrepreneurial College, *Testimony State College* (TSC) has been constantly pressured financially and, at times, the faculty and administrators have thought the state might close the institution. Student applications have consistently increased, and students from throughout the country have applied to the state college, which has somewhat muted the call for closure. Student enrollment is close to 3,000. In-state tuition is about $1200. Over half of the student body is enrolled in arts and humanities. The facilities, although adequate, do not compare with those of EC. However, the natural beauty of the surrounding area at Testimony State is particularly striking.

The president has traditionally spent a good deal of time "fighting off the legislative wolves," although recently it appears that the wolves are at bay. Consequently, the energetic, young new president wants to become involved in the daily life of the college; the faculty are hesitant, if not resistant to the president's advances. The faculty view the administration with a mixture of suspicion and benign neglect. In turn, the administrators respect the faculty even if at times the faculty appear contentious or uninterested in administrative initiatives. The reputation of the faculty as teachers is quite high, and students seem genuinely excited at the interaction between student and teacher. Indeed, the importance of learning and values is one of the essential aspects of the mission.

A longtime faculty member comments, "Our mission is to provide an opportunity for a liberal arts and science education through a delivery system that practices values that are fundamental to a democratic society." An administrator agrees by saying, "Half of the faculty would describe this as a moral curriculum. That's our mission. The way students learn and develop a voice is what makes us different."

In one sense, people first learn about the mission in a manner quite similar to Entrepreneurial College. "I went to AAHE [American Association of Higher Education] and interviewed forty-five people," notes a faculty member, "and almost to a person, every individual said that the ad in the *Chronicle* [*Chronicle for Higher Education*] described the kind of college, the values, that they wanted. And we were the only institution where they had applied."

Another individual describes the process:

Most people talk about research at other interviews, we don't do that. For the people I talk with, they want to teach. The ad self-selects. We explain that teaching is interdisciplinary; we ask people to write an essay on their philosophy of education. We explain that they may be torn in both directions—teaching and research—but that we are a teaching school.

A new faculty member confirms what the speakers say: "I was attracted to the term they used for what I teach—'political economy'—and that they stressed interdisciplinary and multicultural work. Even though we weren't paid to do research, I knew we'd be stimulated by one another."

The difference between Entrepreneurial College and Testimony State is more than one institution writing a better job description about what it does than another (although that is a subject returned to in Chapter 8). The point is that people learn about the distinctiveness of their institution even before they set foot on campus. Once they have arrived on campus their initial impressions are reaffirmed by a host of images and rituals such as parties where faculty give testimony to the specialness of the institution.

An individual who has been at Testimony State for five years observes, "There's a particular way to do things here. Because they had been under the gun so long, there has been a siege mentality built up.

We give particular respect to the people who have survived, to our founding fathers and mothers." Another relatively new person points out, "Look at our catalog. The first thing it says about individual faculty members is the year they came here—not what they teach, not where they got their degree, but the year they came. Doesn't that say it all?" A third person looks at my interview schedule and comments:

I've had an office in every building you're going to today. All of us move our offices every year so that we remain a community. It's a pain in the ass to move every year, but it's a conscious effort, telling us what we do, the importance of collegiality and relating with all of the faculty, not just a chosen few.

I am not suggesting that to strengthen the institution's mission a college president should hold a lottery at the end of every year for faculty to move their offices. Indeed, the example from Testimony State highlights the necessity of contextualizing images and discourse. A proposal to move faculty offices every year on most campuses will meet with much resistance, if not rebellion. At Testimony State the change of offices is in line with the ideology and culture of the institution. On the other hand, a professor also mentions that the first comment about a faculty member in the catalog is how long he or she has served at Testimony and "that says it all." Yet many other institutions also print an individual's length of service at the college and no one pays much attention to the fact. At Testimony State, however, the fact is an important symbolic component of the culture, and the information plays a critical role in helping members define the institution.

It is not coincidental that the examples provided do not have the president's hand in them. Culture does not revolve around an individual. Charisma eventually gets routinized. To be sure, in times of crisis or at the founding of an institution, one's belief in the organization will often be tied to the individual who resides in the president's office. Yet, as Clark notes, "The leader is perishable; he is only one, and increasingly the implementing work is the work of others" (1971, p. 507). Clark's comment is particularly germane at Testimony State. Since its inception Testimony has seen presidents come and go; the "implementing work" has rested largely in the hands of the faculty. Cutting Edge College is also an example of an institution where the culture of the institution has in large part been constructed not by one charismatic individual, but by a large cadre of people—the faculty and administrators.

Usually, the mission evolves organically over time and individuals pay little attention to how it changes. In each of the institutions studied the mission with which the institution began is still in effect. At Christian University the mission is still religious, yet the mission at Christian has changed over time, and the changes often have appeared as struggles by different constituencies over the curriculum. Christian is beset by growing pains that confront many religious colleges and universities. The clientele they once served has either shrunk or other markets have grown.

A parent at Christian University comments that he sent his daughter to the college because, "I believe in the morals that the president espouses here." A younger faculty member hears the statement and says, "What are they? Many of us who are newer, younger, feel that we ought to base our mission on a mission of social justice. We ought to reach out and aid those in need." Another individual says, "Our mission isn't all that clear. A gap exists especially since we serve so many different groups now." As the institution expands in some areas, like its outreach program in continuing education, other areas, such as its undergraduate curriculum, become less clear with regard to the relationship of mission. The point is surely not that the participants should stymie change, but rather to question how change in one area alters the configurations of other areas to the mission.

Women's College (WC) is over 100 years old. The financial footing of the college is secure, and the institutional plant is superb. The tuition is about $10,500. About 40 percent of the 2,500 students enroll in arts and humanities. The student-teacher ratio, about 10 to 1, is the best of the seven institutions under study. Students from throughout the nation attend Women's, and faculty positions are actively sought after. The president is new; many people think the presidency is in a precarious position. People want "leadership" but they do not specify what kind of leadership they want.

Although Women's is better endowed than Christian and has an academically superior student body, more vocal strife appears at Women's College. Some individuals also feel that the distinctiveness of Women's has slipped in recent years. Students and faculty of color are upset with some of the policies of the administration. Women's College still remains a single-sex college, but how individuals interpret the mission of the college has become a source of heated debate.

For example, one traditionally minded faculty member notes: "The debate over our mission is very loud. What does it mean to think of ourselves as a women's college? Some say that it means the curriculum should be different, about women. I think it means women go here. Period." An opposing viewpoint is expressed by an English professor: "Our mission should incorporate scholarship on and by women." An African American professor comments: "Our mission is what we are. We create brilliant Christian women in the Eurocentric tradition."

Each of these examples also points out that an institutional mission is neither static nor universal; yet people are not free to make of it what they will. For example, ideological parameters are set quite firmly at Christian University. "A debate on abortion happened here recently," a professor relates, "but it was unique. We had never thought to have a debate about it before. Everyone knows that it's wrong." Similarly, at Cutting Edge College a professor acknowledges, "We say we want diversity, but not some diversity. A sexist would never make it here. I suppose there are Republicans on the faculty, but you'll never see a contingent for Pat Robertson."

Mission statements, while imposed on all constituencies except those who create them, are both incorporated by individuals and resisted by them. In other words, dominant ideologies, such as that at Christian University, are neither simply handed down from generation to generation, nor are they practiced in a void. On the contrary, an institution's mission is often met with resistance by groups who seek change from the past.

People view the mission from different temporal dimensions, in the context of constituencies, curricula, beliefs, and academic disciplines. For example, at Women's College, the first individual speaks from the viewpoint of the historic past—"We educate women." The second professor speaks from the point of view of advocacy for the future— "We should educate women about women." The third faculty member speaks of the present—"We turn out brilliant Christian women in the Eurocentric tradition." Each of the viewpoints has strong temporal dimensions that affect how the speakers view the overriding ideology of the college. Presumably, a speaker's age, class, racial and sexual orientation, and disciplinary background also affect the way he or she interprets the mission.

Temporal contexts also often influence the way one sees constituencies. Some at Christian University see the institution educating the same group of students they have educated for almost a century—young men and women whose families belong to the religion of the institution. Others see Christian's mission not so much in the light of who attends the college but whom they reach out to help. Still others look at the present demography of the institution and notice that the makeup of Christian is radically different from that of a generation ago; today, men and women of all ages from all religions attend Christian.

Again, the curricula intertwine with the temporal dimensions and constituencies. A mission that teaches scholarship by and about women will be radically different from one that teaches women in a classical tradition. A mission that seeks to meet the needs of diverse constituencies who attend an institution to gain a specific credential will differ from a mission that tries to incorporate the basic teachings of the church into all aspects of learning.

Finally, beliefs about the nature of society and education lead to different viewpoints about the mission. "The mission relates to teaching basic values that are fundamental to a democratic society," notes the individual at Testimony State College. "I have a problem with the idea of building moral education," comments a professor at Women's College. Reflects a professor at Christian University, "I want students to think about the kind of job they'll take when they graduate. That's what our mission is concerned with."

The mission not only sets the parameters of discourse, but also permeates activities throughout the organization—even by its absence. Entrepreneurial College outwardly allows for a variety of activities by the looseness of its mission; yet because participants have a weak definition of the mission, when an action such as the denial of tenure occurs, individuals no longer casually converse as much as they once did.

Testimony State stresses interaction with students and does not condone faculty work that focuses on research activities to the detriment of student contact. Certain forms of classroom interaction seem to run contrary to the mission of the institution. "A successful teacher here," notes an academic administrator, "will not teach as he or she does at other institutions." "There's a way to do things. I was treated as if I had never taught before," comments a professor. A new professor reflects, "I have to keep telling myself not to lecture, 'to seminar'— it's a verb here—that that is tied into the nature of this college."

At Women's College people who resist change are known as "dinosaurs." Even the "dinosaurs" use the term about themselves. One professor has an inflatable dinosaur sitting on his office bookshelf. He explains the term by saying, "The politics of pedagogy is very evident here. If you're not a traditionalist like I am then you think that the lecture is elitist and discussion is central. I believe there is value in lecturing, in getting across the facts to young people." "Someone started a rumor," another individual bemusedly states, "that the feminists in the administration building were taking all the lecture podiums out of the classrooms so that the faculty would not be able to lecture anymore."

Thus, even inert objects on one campus such as lecture podiums become highly charged symbols on another campus. I noted previously how moving everyone's office yearly at Testimony State represents a specific symbolic meaning whereas the same action on a campus such as Entrepreneurial College would most likely foment resistance. Groups relate objects and discourses to particular images that are in some way tied to the ideological nature of the institution's mission. What remains to be discussed in this chapter is how different interpretations of the mission come about, and how one evaluates whether the mission is doing what it says.

CONSTRUCTING AND EVALUATING MISSIONS

The above examples demonstrate how the interpretation of the mission depends upon historical precedence as enacted in institutional procedures and policies and the present contextual surroundings in which the organization finds itself. Both the procedures and policies and the contextual surroundings exist as consequences of power. As defined previously, power does not reside in the hands of one man or woman, but as a multitude of tactics and strategies that create possibilities for positive and negative moments.

As a negative example, junior faculty feel disenfranchised from Entrepreneurial and perceive themselves as helpless. No one is able to turn the denial of tenure into a debate about the mission of the institution. Instead, different constituencies seek to reaffirm the ambiguity—we have not changed. Another example concerns the words, and ultimate action, of an African American professor at Women's College. An education in the "Eurocentric tradition" appears overwhelming to some concerned faculty and administrators to such an extent that they feel powerless to change the system. During the course of the year the

African American professor and two additional African American administrators and faculty announce their intentions to leave Women's College.

As a positive movement, I offer the examples of constituencies struggling over how to define what they are about; participants in Christian University create different definitions for what the mission should be. Different groups no longer accept that the mission exists to the exclusion of clientele other than the traditional age group who are Christian. Faculty at Cutting Edge and Testimony State consistently debate and argue about "who we are." And even though at Women's College some constituencies feel powerless, other groups have brought critical questions into focus about the nature of the mission and curriculum. Questions that were never important before, such as what it means to be a women's institution, are now common debates and dialogues among all sectors of the college.

Women's College brings to the forefront specific symbols of domination or liberation. In some areas of campus, discourse about the mission of the institution does not occur, protecting the assumption that everyone similarly interprets "what this place is about." In other areas of the campus, people seek to expose the underpinnings of an educational mission that is Eurocentric, or male-centered. Except in institutions in crisis or revolution, organizational participants work with *pieces* of problems, one step at a time. Organizational life is a process out of which goals arise and are reached. Through the confluence of context, individual initiative and the culture of the organization, different discourses arise and disappear. The cacophony and struggle over the mission that Women's College displays points toward the empowerment of groups. One of the difficulties for some participants involved in the process is to confuse disagreement with defeat. One of the disappointments for other participants is to acknowledge that other voices still remain silenced.

Testimony State College makes its mission explicit in its recruitment policies; yet the college also attracts people who will oppose a hegemonic voice. The institution, seeking polyphony within the parameters of its mission, incorporates alternative views. The voices, discourse, struggle, debate, continues unabated. "We know what we're doing," says one, "and we will continue to tear it down so that things are exposed, so that our discussion is clear." Other faculty concur that they do not want to maintain the status quo. If anything, the status quo at Testimony State implies perpetual *change*.

The examples point out how individuals consistently contest the idea that a mission is an ideological given to be accepted by all constituencies. Forms of alternative discourse appear that challenge the previous order. Voices arise that suggest that the mission as it was previously stated either is inappropriate or no longer meets the needs of different constituencies. What occurs is not only a bringing into question whether the institution is achieving its mission, but also whether the mission itself is appropriate. The approach used for understanding whether the mission is working is more often informal and ongoing rather than formal and temporary. Except in times of crisis, when the organization must decide to take one avenue or another, the evaluation of the mission occurs incrementally and without formal discussion. To be sure, accreditation agencies will call for dialogue about the nature of the institution when an accreditation visit is due; but, more often than not, such dialogues take place to say that they *have* taken place. The assumption is that organizational participants give most credence to the ongoing analysis and evaluation of the mission.

For example, an administrator at Testimony State College comments on how she knows the institution is achieving its mission by saying, "There's no one way, really. You have to get out and talk to people, you have to see what's being done." The AVP at Testimony adds, "You can tell by the extent to which we have been able to conserve the energy and direction of the college while adapting to changing realities like rapid growth and internationalism."

"I don't know how you do it, managerially," concludes an African American woman at Women's College. "But I'll tell you this: this college is very ineffective when it comes to meeting the needs of people of color. The college doesn't even see the problem." However, a male professor at the college states, "We decided years ago we wanted to be multicultural. It's sincere, but inept. There's no way we can say we are achieving our mission when you evaluate it by any common standards of quality."

Presumably, the "people" with whom Testimony State College will choose to talk are different than those at Christian University. It is also a mere truism that different constituencies within an institution will talk with different people, as evidenced by the two individuals at Women's

College. One individual presumably looks to students of color to see if the college meets its mission; and the other looks to the curriculum and standard tests to see if students comprehend what is taught.

The academic vice president at Testimony State speaks of "realities"; yet growth or decrease in enrollment is more than simply a "reality" (Tierney, 1987). The markets to which institutions reach out or those markets that do not respond in some part are constructed by the participants in the institution. For example, Christian University has responded to nondenominational markets that have requested services. Is the institution meeting its mission? "We need a clearer sense of institutional purpose before I can respond," comments one professor. "We have a new thrust—the adult learner—and people won't recognize it. Our mission is still back in the evangelical concept," observes another individual.

A professor notes that Women's College is effective at providing a "brilliant Eurocentric education"; but adds, "If we are serious about cultural diversity—to serve women of all colors—then we need to realize the serious deficiencies." Another professor contradicts that contention: "I think students should have a common body of knowledge. I like Hirsch's book, *Cultural Literacy*, and feel we can do the same for higher education, if that's what we want to do."

Each comment points out how people constantly evaluate whether the institution fulfills its mission. Different voices arise and different evaluations are given. The decision about which criteria to choose, who will make the choices, and what components of the program to evaluate, all have the ability to raise ideological tensions. The question for organizational participants is how to utilize the tensions so that the institution comes to grips with discordant discourses. The temptation for the participants is either to mask or to ignore the discord.

Five institutions have been presented. Cutting Edge College, Testimony State, Christian University, Entrepreneurial College, and Women's College all have built different cartographies of their institutional landscapes. The participants at each institution also interpret the topography of each institution differently. What are we to make of so many conflicting conceptions of what a mission is, how it is to be evaluated, and how it changes?

Clearly, people do make sense of their organizational lives in relation to the mission of the institution. The mission provides guidance, not only on grand scales, such as whether the institution should emphasize teaching or research, but also on more microscopic levels, such as whether a professor should lecture at a podium or conduct a seminar. Ideological tensions constantly arise as people interpret the mission in a manner differently than intended. We now turn to the main battleground where the interpretation of the mission is contested—the curriculum—and I introduce the final two institutions—Working Class State College and Classics College.

4

Institutional Topography: The Curriculum

The etymology of curriculum derives from "curricle," a two-wheeled carriage or racing chariot. Originally intended to define a racecourse, the word has been appropriated to connote a course of study or training. How educators have defined what the course of study or training should be has varied remarkably throughout the history of American higher education. In *The Reforming of General Education*, Daniel Bell stated the question in the following manner: "Is it the task of the university to be a clerisy, self-consciously guarding the past and seeking assertively to challenge the new? Or is it just a bazaar, offering Coleridge and Blake, Burckhardt and Nietzsche, Weber and Marx as antiphonal prophets, each with his own call?" (1967, p. 348).

What counts for knowledge and how organizational participants decide what knowledge to include in the curriculum are the focal points of this chapter. By looking at the nature of knowledge and how definitions of knowledge do or do not get incorporated into the curriculum, we will consider whose interests the curriculum reflects as well as those who are not heard with regard to curricular change.

KNOWLEDGE, CULTURE, AND THE CURRICULUM

This section will further delve into the curriculum and construction of knowledge at Cutting Edge College and Entrepreneurial College.

First, however, we will discuss an institution with a quite different conception of what accounts for knowledge from both Cutting Edge and Entrepreneurial. The institution has a long history of teaching "the classics." By and large, the *Classics College* (CC) faculty do not conduct research; teaching is paramount. Classics has prided itself on its student body; although competition to get into the college is not terrifically competitive, the student makeup ranks Classics as one of the best in the country. Established over 80 years ago, half of the students graduate within four years. Retaining the other students has become a major concern. Student enrollment is slightly over 1,000, and FTE faculty is around 100. However, faculty fear that they are not getting the kind of students they once had.

Over the years Classics has had several difficult periods balancing the budget; but they seem to have weathered the storm, primarily through the president's fund-raising efforts and slightly larger class sizes. The administration is small, and the faculty wish it were smaller. After a long tenure at Classics, the president is about to step down, and the AVP will retire soon after. Rumors abound that the new president will want an academic vice president from the outside—a departure from tradition. Several "living legends" of the faculty will also soon retire. Retirements may mean that the purpose of Classics will change, and change has been adamantly resisted by the faculty. The purpose of the institution has always been clear to most of the faculty: "We believe we are an educational institution," mentions one long-time faculty member, "and not a social hostel, or a training program to get along with people, or a 'how to' vocational school. We are dedicated to education." By education, the professor means that students must have a firm understanding of Western civilization.

A student describes what he thinks about the curriculum: "They really make you think. I've learned so much about my past, about Western culture and society. It's intense. Sometimes I think it's too bad we don't learn about other cultures, but you can't learn everything. I feel I'm getting a well-rounded education."

Other students echo his feelings. "Sure, . . . the Eurocentric idea," says one, "this is Eurocentric. But we live in America." "We need to know where we come from," adds another. "I didn't want spoon-feeding. I really wanted to investigate knowledge," comments a third student. To most students at Classics, knowledge is what the curriculum

is about; students do not learn skills, or job training, or ethical values;
they learn to think and to understand the nature of knowledge.

Although Classics has remained relatively true to its roots in a classical curriculum, the institution is undergoing a minor upheaval.
Younger faculty have been hired who have different ideas about the
curriculum and the role of faculty. A faculty member who has recently
arrived and has teaching experience elsewhere, shakes her head, saying:

I'm shocked at how very old-fashioned notions exist. Greeks and Romans and
Christians. I'm amazed there's such a slow process. I'm still astonished that
the symposium isn't taught. We are intellectually out of date. And we talk
about interdisciplinary work, but it's a joke when I think about other places
I've been.

Interdisciplinary coursework at Classics means that faculty from different disciplines give a lecture in the humanities course required for
all students. "There's no synthesis going on," says a humanities professor, "There's no dialogue across the disciplines. One individual
comes into class and does his thing, and then the next week another
person comes in and does his thing." At Classics the departments are
quite strong, and most innovation occurs with regard to the major.
Although suggestions have been made to reform the overall curriculum,
no changes have been forthcoming either through apathy or contentment.
"We don't have a structure, a process, for bringing about change,"
comments one faculty member. A younger faculty member adds, "We
don't have any leaders here. The president is a banker president, the
AVP is a paper pusher, and the old guard don't see any problems. They
want to preserve the past." A member of the "old guard" acknowledges, "We haven't gone in for fads. We've stayed the same because
we're right."

The president reflects on his tenure and the state of the curriculum.
He expresses chagrin and disappointment. "We have not done a good
enough job with the curriculum. We have what we once had, and little
more. New ideas don't come easily. To get this faculty to move, to
act, is almost an impossibility." A senior faculty member concurs,
"We are extremely conservative. We were innovative fifty years ago,
and haven't been ever since."

Given the faculty's disdain for "fads," many of the recent critics of higher education could find much that they like about the curriculum at Classics. Allan Bloom has noted, "Every educational system has a moral goal that it tries to attain and that informs its curriculum. It wants to produce a certain kind of human being" (1987, p. 26). From this perspective a collegiate curriculum is the vehicle for informing the young about the nature of the society in which we live. For Americans, relevant knowledge to be included in a college curriculum concerns the history of Western civilization. Rather than open the curriculum to a mélange of knowledge as if society had no specific anchoring points, recent critics and senior faculty at Classics College believe the curriculum exists in relation to the received traditions of American society. Again, Bloom is helpful in elaborating on this idea: "I have heard the abandonment of requirements to learn languages or philosophy or science lauded as a progress of openness. . . . To be open to knowing, there are certain kinds of things one must know" (1987, p. 41). The idea is that there is a unity to knowledge and one of the purposes of the curriculum is to provide the essential building blocks of knowledge so that people are free to think.

"That idea is absurd," states a young professor in the humanities. "They're against 'isms,' which usually means feminism." In the words of Schuster and Van Dyne, what is occurring at Classics is that faculty teach from an "invisible paradigm" (1984) where knowledge is removed from the context in which it is situated. From this perspective the lives of women, people of color, and sexual minorities are marginalized and trivialized. The invisible paradigm is the sum of the curricular offerings that constitute knowledge. Knowledge, then, is neither neutral nor objective. Instead, what counts for knowledge is a social construction that embodies particular groups' assumptions about the way the world is built.

Recently, organizational participants at many institutions have further incorporated minority authors into reading lists, or a course has been offered to supplement the "regular" curriculum. Such additions have been attacked from two directions. On the one hand, people such as William Bennett find it spurious to include writers simply because of their color or gender. A senior professor at Classics concurs: "Let's be realistic. There just weren't that many black writers or women writers around in the past. But that doesn't mean we add someone to the humanities core just because he's black any more than we should add someone because he's white."

On the other hand, many politically active faculty resent the idea that adding "an author or two" will solve any of the problems about which they speak. "Everything remains the same," comments one professor at Classics. "We provide the same framework, the same values and practices." The canon of what society knows as knowledge may have been revised to include a new author; but the assumptions about the nature of knowledge and how curricula are built and justified remain the same. Colleges want to graduate well-rounded individuals. In other words, to be well-rounded in the waning days of the twentieth century— at Classics College—means essentially what it did 50 years ago, except that a few different authors are on reading lists.

Thus, the argument has revolved around how discourses are produced, received, and interpreted, instead of first asking why particular discourses occur and others do not. Daniel Bell's quotation at the start of this chapter highlights my point. He poses the dichotomy that the curriculum *either* "guards the past" *or* is a "bazaar" for the new. The senior faculty at Classics are examples of guardians of tradition, and those who fight to add women or minority authors to a syllabus are proponents of the "bazaar." If I borrowed an analogy from sports, I might say that the argument should be about the ground rules of curricular structures, as well as who can play.

Another way of phrasing the argument is to question not the content of the curriculum, but the structures themselves. The question then becomes, how do the organizational participants refocus the discussion away from one of enlightenment, where students learn to be well educated, to a discussion of empowerment that questions what kinds of students are produced by these curricula. Rather than assume that knowledge is a cultural list of facts and figures which faculty can either add to or subtract from, I consider knowledge as a social product with political consequences. As Zavarzadeh and Morton note, such a notion enables

the student to see that his or her understanding of all of culture's texts (from philosophical treatises to popular television shows) is a result of situatedness in a complex network of gender, class and race relations and to see that reading (and meaning) changes depending on whether the reader is a male or female reader, a Hispanic or white American reader, a working-class reader or upper-class reader. (1987, p. 19)

The question, then, is not who to put on a reading list, but rather, how the list is conceived and used. The importance of knowledge concerns how it helps students understand the situation and context in which they are embedded, and unmasks the particular interests and assumptions at work in society. To see the implications of this fusion of knowledge and curriculum, we return to Cutting Edge College.

At Cutting Edge, interdisciplinary work is essential, and departmental boundaries do not exist. Instead, the faculty teach in separate schools and act as cross-fertilizers for one another. At Cutting Edge it is more common to see an individual trained in English literature working and co-teaching with someone in economics or biology than it is to see three English faculty teaching a course. As one individual explains, "I put together a course and then one or two of my colleagues go over it. They really make me rethink it, too! Sometimes I will drop in on someone's course just to pick up something people are doing that I don't know about."

What makes the comment interesting is that the individuals he refers to are from areas other than his own; the courses he speaks of sitting in on are not in his discipline. Another individual adds, "What's really special about Cutting Edge is the frequency with which we drop in on one another and discuss what we're doing, our ideas, our concerns." People constantly refer to how they "drop in on" and talk with one another about their courses and intellectual dilemmas. Another person confirms the interdisciplinary nature of Cutting Edge: "The institution gives you the freedom and space and help to make connections across boundaries. Your concerns and interests affect you on a curricular level, on what you teach."

What kind of coherence can be made out of a curricular structure that looks on the face of it as if it exists by whim or fancy? At Classics College, for example, professors have intellectual "buckets" that guide the kind of curriculum that will be developed. A biochemistry professor at Classics explains, "The nature of my discipline, the knowledge in it, is being developed so fast. We don't do interdisciplinary things here because just to keep up in my discipline is next to impossible." Although the professor is in a discipline that many look upon as a hybrid—biology and chemistry—the individual speaks quite clearly about what guides his thinking about what kind of knowledge needs to inform the curriculum. Faculty members identify with their discipline, which in turn defines what will be taught. The assumption follows Bloom's line of thinking; students need to be socialized—"there are certain things one must know"—and the discipline defines what those "things" are.

What guides Cutting Edge's curricular process? Various faculty members speak about the purpose of their curriculum in terms that are antithetical to the notion of knowledge as facts and figures. "We believe that in general disciplinary knowledge is the product of a historical accident," comments one person. "We need to explode the myth that someone can master a concrete entity called 'knowledge,' " adds another. One longtime faculty member adds, "I think we should take the curriculum apart every few years, totally start over, so that we don't fool ourselves." Another individual comments:

The curriculum is fragmented, purposefully so. People need to cut it up into different pieces, take knowledge apart and put it back together again. We want students to make the synthesis and connections for themselves. Somewhere after World War II it became impossible to think of all knowledge existing in one paradigm. We're in a different world now and we want to enable our students to grasp onto the power structures. Our purpose isn't just to teach Caribbean literature, but to teach people how to read.

Although most who teach at Cutting Edge agree with the curricular goals, some people are also concerned that not enough structure exists. "I'm dissatisfied with the process," admits one individual. "The curriculum is not coherent because we start out with faculty preference and then leave it up to the students to make the connections. That's not good." Says another, "I don't believe in rigid formulations, but this is too loose sometimes, and the student who is not in command of his or her life gets lost."

A new faculty member speaks about the difficulty that occurs with this curricular approach by talking about her teaching: "We call it 'mode of inquiry,' because we don't lecture, we want discussion. In general I like it, but I worry sometimes that they're missing something. I think my students should know about the Licensing Act of 1737, but how do I get that across?"

Presumably the speaker's concern is not only that students learn about a law concerning the theater, but also about other information as well. Her concern is similar to that of the science professor at Classics College: "What do students need to know?" The difference in curricular formulas between Classics and Cutting Edge is that the former assumes all well-educated people must know certain data, whereas the latter denies the assumption that knowledge is ever neutral. Futhermore, Classics College assumes that until one masters particular information one will not be able to think independently. The outcome of an education is the ability to think. At Cutting Edge College, conversely, they assume that mastery of knowledge is a subjective task that must be understood as a political undertaking. Critical inquiry is the subject of learning.

In one way, Entrepreneurial College is similar to Classics' conception of knowledge. Entrepreneurial has a potpourri of innovative programs that faculty have devised. Some students spend their freshman year together studying a particular set of courses. Other students take a more traditional body of courses. Additional students spend an intensive amount of time in one course. And still other students become immediately involved in their majors to meet the rigorous demands of premedical degrees or engineering and the like. Although the faculty do not agree that one body of knowledge must be taught, the faculty are similar to Classics in the sense that in general they work from the assumption that what they teach is value-neutral. One individual, for example, says: "I'm involved in the freshmen seminar, and it really shakes students up, they really end up questioning what they're all about. But I honestly don't care what they believe. We don't teach one ideological stance here. Students can pick and choose, and we're quite open about it."

In the spring I interview four students who turn out to be "political conservatives." I ask them if they feel particular points of view are being taught. They laugh and nod their heads as one student explains:

In some classes it doesn't matter, like science or engineering. In some classes it does matter, like Latin American Studies or Political Science. That's where the really liberal faculty are, but they're very open about what they believe and we're free to disagree and debate them. I like having them tell their side of the story so I can be prepared when I get out in the real world to defeat the kind of crazy ideas they have. So I'd say they have an ideology, but it's not doctrinaire or anything. It's just a typical liberal professor. But they are open to debate.

Entrepreneurial College's approach to learning is in line with its mission that allows for faculty to define their relationship to the institution in a wide variety of manners. The shared conviction of the mission is the belief that faculty have the freedom to teach whatever they want;

the design and conduct of the curriculum reflects the diversity. Given that the faculty have the freedom of definition, the assumption is that the approaches to learning, and hence knowledge and the curriculum, is diversified and abstract. Like Classics and unlike Cutting Edge, Entrepreneurial's faculty do not have an overriding ideology that governs what they teach; instead, they have more of a smorgasbord approach to learning. Unlike Classics, the faculty at Entrepreneurial do not believe that all students must learn a particular canon of knowledge.

The way the faculty know at Classics College if a student has mastered his or her subject matter is through a senior thesis. In general the thesis is discipline-based, and interaction occurs between the student and one thesis advisor. A long-time faculty member points out, "It's nice to know that the rest of the world is catching on to what we've been doing. People like Boyer now say that a senior thesis is a good form of assessment."

Cutting Edge College has no cultural literacy test for its students. In fact, faculty and administrators seem relatively unconcerned with an overall assessment. Instead, they believe that constant monitoring and advising of students, different thesislike projects during a student's career, and the interaction students have in classes and with their committees provides good evidence about what the student has or has not learned. The projects are in some ways the *anti*-thesis of Classics projects. The projects must cross disciplines, and work occurs not just with one professor but a small team. Interestingly, both Classics and Cutting Edge have final products that are similar to honor's or thesis papers; the process each institution takes to reach the goal of a final paper, however, is radically different, which in turn, effects the purpose of the goal. Classics' goal is to show that a student has mastered a specific body of knowledge, whereas Cutting Edge's goal is to enable the student to understand the underpinnings of the social construction of knowledge. Entrepreneurial College has a more traditional approach to the assessment of learning. Different faculty have different conceptions of what to test students on, and final exams and term papers provide ongoing analyses; there is no unified attempt to have all students either write a senior thesis or undertake a particular project.

Another way to think about assessing what students learn is to also think about what students do not learn. What kind of learning occurs at Classics College that does not take place at Cutting Edge College or

Entrepreneurial? What is similar? How do the different faculties account for the other?

As already noted, at Classics the curriculum is prescribed and based on Western civilization, or "Eurocentric," as the student commented. "Women don't fit in our curriculum," notes one student. "Sexism is a problem we won't own up to," comments another. "Male teachers teaching male texts. And guess who gets called on most in class?" A male student acknowledges that men dominate class discussion but says, "Everybody's free to speak up, speak out. That's what is great about our seminars. I don't like sexism, but what can you do? We didn't invent it; we can't solve it."

Pieces of the knowledge puzzle begin to fit together at Classics College. Knowledge is objective and students are made to think about how they can best understand it. Because of the knowledge explosion within each discipline there is much emphasis on disciplinary rigor. Students are not taught to see themselves as part of the process which they study. Sexism, Eurocentrism and the like are acknowledged, but they are not brought into a discourse that links what the student learns with how the world is built.

Similarly, at Entrepreneurial students are taught in some courses to think about concepts such as sexism or racism; but the curriculum does not have an overarching concern with how knowledge is produced or why particular subjects are studied and others not. Instead, Entrepreneurial follows its general mission that allows for a diversified approach to learning where students come into contact with quite different conceptions of faculty beliefs about what counts for knowledge. Some of Entrepreneurial's faculty would fit well in Classics College, and others would be more suited to Cutting Edge.

At Cutting Edge College, people acknowledge that students can graduate from the institution without having come into contact with certain subjects or authors. A professor ruminates, "Does it bother me that a student can graduate without enough coursework in the sciences, or that a kid might not have dabbled enough in the quantitative area? To be honest with you, yes, it bothers me. Should we do anything about it, such as change requirements, absolutely not." Other faculty concur with the professor. "A curriculum will never be a hundred percent error-free," comments one. "A curriculum is a philosophy, and because we don't always achieve it, doesn't mean we should abandon it," adds another. In general, the feeling seems to be that because a student misses an opportunity to broaden his or her horizon does not mean that the process is flawed; if anything, it means that a better advising system is needed.

From the standpoint of the faculty and the students, all institutions need better advising systems. "Advising is terrible," grumbles a student at Classics College; "you can never find your adviser and when you do he doesn't know any more than you do." A student at Entrepreneurial complains: "Faculty don't care about advising. They don't know how to do it, spend the time, actually counsel people. It's especially bad for freshmen. There's so much to take here, but you never learn how to do it." A student at Cutting Edge adds, "It's hit-and-miss. It can take you a long time to find the person who's right for you. And because we work closely with faculty on the exams, it can be frightening."

An area where Classics and Cutting Edge and, to an extent, Entrepreneurial converge is that of the method of instruction. Unlike Women's College where lecture podiums have caused a stir, Classics and Cutting Edge place a high premium on seminars with maximum student interaction. As might be expected, at Entrepreneurial some faculty feel the lecture is the best method, and others believe seminars are better. The difference between the pedagogic styles of Classics and Cutting Edge concerns the overall goals of the curriculum at both institutions. At Classics College a student says excitedly, "You get going in one of those seminars and boy it's fantastic! They really make you think in there. You really feel great ideas are being discussed and you're part of the debate."

One night at Cutting Edge I have supper with a student in a campus restaurant; he greets me at the front door dressed in a bright red beret, a faded T-shirt and jeans. As we sit at the rooftop cafe he speaks of his life at the college:

I'm made to question where I fit in the grand scheme of things. I constantly am brought back to myself, to my relationship to what we're learning. I never thought it would be so lonely. . . . The way it's structured you work incredibly hard on your own. Work. Work. Work. I'm always in the library, or perhaps talking to a professor. It's not an easy life, but I'm learning a lot. What this place teaches you is how to get your hands on the knowledge, to access knowledge.

Again, the inherent differences of each approach come out. The seminar at Classics encourages students to objectify knowledge and see if they can make sense of the knowledge they are taught. The Cutting Edge seminar tries to make students see how what is being discussed impacts on their lives. At Classics College whether the knowledge is referentially linked to the student's life is serendipitous. At Cutting Edge College knowledge is always contextual. At Entrepreneurial students may be exposed to both forms of learning, but as the individual stated above, knowledge is not viewed as ideological. Thus, the curriculum is removed from unearthing the underpinnings of what counts for knowledge. Students may be taught different theories or political viewpoints, but in general they still come to see knowledge as objective.

The student's comment about loneliness should also be mentioned. Each of the institutions value the intellect, but the manner in which the participants manifest that value differs between Cutting Edge and Classics on the one hand, and Entrepreneurial on the other. At Classics and Cutting Edge words like "rigor," "intense," and "standards" continually crop up in conversations with the different constituencies. As opposed to many other institutions in America, and at Entrepreneurial, not much effort is expended toward a student's socio-emotional needs at Cutting Edge or Classics. At Classics they disdain it—"we're not a social hostel," commented the professor. At Cutting Edge their energies are directed elsewhere. A new student services administrator comments, "People say there's no community here; that there are a lot of isolated individuals. To a certain extent that's true. We don't put enough emphasis on the emotional side of things."

In many respects the culture of Cutting Edge and Classics has created what the participants view as legitimate knowledge. "It's important for us to be cutting-edge," says an individual at the institution, pointing out one of the key precepts of the college. Institutional culture highlights particular pieces of knowledge which the participants seek to legitimate and, as importantly, subsumes other knowledge forms that remain hidden or discredited. Because Entrepreneurial has a diffuse culture as derived from the mission, what gets defined as legitimate knowledge is also diffuse. At Entrepreneurial some students join fraternities and the football team—the antithesis of student life at Cutting Edge and Classics—and other students disdain such activities. Entrepreneurial values the intellect, but not to the exclusion of students' socio-emotional needs that extend beyond the classroom.

Working from the notion of culture developed in Chapter 2, I have tried to point out how ideology is enacted through curricular formations.

Three institutions where the fit between ideology and discourse is relatively tight have been considered. Although the ideologies and the curricular formations of each institution are quite different, within the culture a relatively high degree of consistency exists. We turn now to a discussion of how curricular decisions get made.

CURRICULAR DECISIONS AND ORGANIZATIONAL CULTURE

Working Class State College (WCSC) will provide a fresh perspective insofar as the institution is quite different from Entrepreneurial, Classics, and Cutting Edge. The coherence of the curriculum and the mission evidenced at Classics, Cutting Edge, and Entrepreneurial is not readily apparent at Working Class State. The institution is like many others—a normal school begun after the Civil War that changed to a teacher's college, then a college, and now has the unsure status of a university. Student enrollment is over 2,000. As a public institution it is part of a state system with a faculty of almost 200 that has a collective bargaining agreement. Working Class has an aging faculty, many of whom will retire within the next five years. Most students come from throughout the state, although the preponderance are regional sons and daughters. The president has "swept house" and the top administration is almost entirely new.

Because Working Class is part of a state system, it has environmental pressures and constraints that Cutting Edge and Classics do not. Yet it also has the latitude to create the kind of institution it wants to be. "I think we should become the best public institution in the state," says a new administrator. "We didn't use any of the old documents or histories when we were writing our mission statement," confides Working Class's chair of the accreditation report. "We're deciding now what we want to be in the future." "We excel in international studies and I think we should play that up more," comments another individual. "There are untapped markets out there waiting for us, if we're willing to get off our butts," adds a fourth person.

In large part, however, what they say they want the institution to become—the mission—has not made an impact on the curriculum. For example, Working Class perceives itself as a force in international studies because the state has designated international studies as a specialty area at WCSC. In reality, the extent of the specialty is a smattering of programs abroad. Roughly 10 percent of the student body utilize the program for a semester or a year. When they return, few students major in international studies, and no one seems able to provide any tangible evidence or idea about what kind of learning goes on during the student's year abroad. One individual says, "The experience of students is just amazing. They say they've learned a lot, and other professors comment how good it is to have one in their classes. It's just an amazing program." A faculty member concurs, "You can always tell a kid who's been abroad. They speak up." And a third individual adds, "I know they enjoy it, that it's a good thing. I'm glad they get the opportunity." The vagueness of responses reflects the uncertainty of goals.

It is certainly possible to think that the college would not emphasize a program that involves such a small percentage of the student body—10 percent. "It's our jewel in the crown," contends one individual. What becomes apparent, however, is that at Working Class the curriculum is a static entity. As opposed to Entrepreneurial College, which changes when someone gets a feasible idea, the constituencies of Working Class State College have appeared short on ideas other than modest tinkering here and there.

But the winds of change are upon the institution. The new administrative team is determined to implement a vast array of proposals; one individual wants to implement an international studies major. Another person wants a modified honors program. An additional person wants a more coherent core program. Teaching loads and decisions over who gets sabbaticals and how they are apportioned out also have become critical issues with some individuals; some people teach relatively few classes and others teach many. The appearance is that the college has no rationale for the discrepancies. Sabbaticals seem to be doled out with little thought given to what a faculty member will accomplish during the sabbatical; instead, it appears that the college offers a sabbatical to the individual who is next in line in terms of length of service. Clearly, the agenda for change is full; whether the faculty will allow such changes to occur is an open question. In the fall, for example, the academic vice president tried to change the registration process and encountered stiff resistance from many corners of the faculty.

Another question concerns what the curriculum will be called upon to do. Working Class State resides in an area with a high unemployment rate and little idea of how to stem the economic depression that besets the city. Union workers have gone on strike at a factory, and management has replaced them. For all intents and purposes, it appears after more than a year's strike that the workers have lost their jobs. Management has no intention of hiring the workers back. New industry is not coming into the area; instead, small businesses are leaving the town.

Most people credit the president of Working Class State with improving the town-gown relationship. "Everybody attends his Christmas party," relates one faculty member. "He's at so many of our social events, that he's really like one of us," notes a citizen of the town. Yet for all of the socializing, little educational relationship of a critical nature takes place between the town and WCSC. One citizen says "If we want a course in photography or painting or something we can just call up continuing education and they'll try to get it for us." However, an unemployed worker says, "The college doesn't help. They walk a fine line because they don't want to piss management off. We need retraining, some type of economic development plan, but the college isn't interested. We don't know what to do." Another local worker says, "You'd think because the faculty is in a union that they'd support us, but they don't. They don't have anything to do with us up there in their ivory tower."

Is it the duty of a public state college to cater to a local clientele in its curriculum? Not necessarily. Testimony State College, for example, attracts students from all over the state. Yet it appears at Working-Class State that curricular decisions are made with little reference to either ideological assessment or a discourse that actively interprets the organization's culture. Ostensibly, the state founded public institutions to serve the needs of the citizens and the state. To be sure, how one interprets who the citizens are, and who makes up the state, will vary dramatically depending upon one's background and interests. The unemployed worker mentioned above has succinctly pointed out one interpretation. If the faculty were to be actively involved with the strike, the business leaders would undoubtedly feel that the college was not serving the needs of the state and the college was hindering economic development and the growth of business. Conversely, by the faculty's silence, the strikers seem to feel that Working-Class State is not speaking in their interests. Either way, how faculty and administrators act toward the community—how they define words such as "community"—are assessments of the relationship between college and community. What is not apparent at Working-Class State is the awareness that such assessments are taking place.

When asked how they assess the curriculum, individuals respond in the following way: "Do our students get jobs? That's the question to ask, and the answer is yes." A second person comments, "We've changed so that kids get jobs." Note how different these responses are from those of the other two institutions discussed in this chapter. Classics College has a senior thesis that supposedly enables the faculty to judge something about the character of a student's intellectual capabilities. The faculty at Cutting Edge College say it is not concerned with a single-assessment tool and prefer ongoing evaluations that inform them about a student's critical thinking. Entrepreneurial College has the faculty assess students in an ongoing manner. Working Class State College takes the assessment out of the hands of the faculty and puts it into the hands of employers. Obviously, all institutions concern themselves with whether their students get jobs. And Working Class also gives grades in classes in a manner quite similar to Entrepreneurial. However, the emphasis and perception is different at Working Class than at the other three schools. Only at Working Class did the faculty mention jobs as the key assessment. The other institutions continually spoke about their definition of knowledge and how they assessed it. At Working Class the assessment tool has little, if anything, to do with knowledge as the other institutions have defined it; rather, knowledge concerns skill development.

Similarly, the frontispiece for the curriculum is general education. "We're so far out of step we're back in step," says one faculty member proudly. The requirements that the individual speaks of are 60 credits scattered across the curriculum. "It's really just a laundry list," admits one fellow, "political trade-offs so everyone is happy." A new faculty member complains, "There's no coherence in any of this. We don't get an overall picture of what it's supposed to mean." The "overall picture" is another way to describe an ideological assessment and an active interpretation of the organization's culture.

The question to be raised here is the influence of society in determining the ideological apparatus of the institution that defines what a curriculum will be, how it will be evaluated, and who will evaluate it. At a public institution that educates primarily working-class students, the curriculum revolves around preparation for the work world. At

Entrepreneurial College, Classics College, or Cutting Edge College students do not gain a hold of knowledge that ostensibly prepares them for the world of work. Instead, even though the institutions differ about how to define knowledge, they evidently provide students with an introduction to how conceptual systems operate, rather than specific technical knowledge.

The differences in class background between the students of Working Class State and the other three institutions demand comment. In general, the students of Classics and Cutting Edge come from similar backgrounds—upper middle-class neighborhoods. The Entrepreneurial student body is the wealthiest of the seven institutions under study. The students of WSCS come from and will return to working-class towns and cities. How faculty form the curriculum and what they believe knowledge is certainly takes into account the composition of the student body. The relationship of the organization's culture to its environment takes on increased importance. How the organizational participants reinforce, contradict, or expose the underpinnings of that relationship gets acted out in discourses on the terrain of the curriculum. In many respects, the faculties of Cutting Edge, Classics, and Entrepreneurial assume their students will get jobs. The same assumption cannot be made at Working Class, which in turn affects all aspects of the curriculum. Note the difference with regard to how four faculty talk about how the curriculum is shaped in the following discussion at Cutting Edge College.

Faculty #1: The disciplines give us no clues, no help whatsoever.

Faculty #2: If I published in my field, in the *American Political Science Review*, people around here would say, "That's too bad!"

Faculty #3: I don't know what it would be like if we couldn't work with one another. The reward is in the ability to work with other faculty.

Faculty #4: There's a collegiality that's forced on you. Sure, we fight and yell, just like a family. But I'm stunned at how many people are alienated elsewhere.

Faculty #3: The collegiality is just great. I went to a women's studies dinner the other night. I wouldn't do that if I were at another place.

Faculty #1: You need an intellectual center of gravity to create a curriculum, and people have relied on the disciplines for that, but now the disciplines are dead.

Faculty #2: To some extent, we create our own cutting edge.

Faculty #4: I hope in the future we work out a few more coherent courses of study. Feminist Studies, Law . . .

Faculty #3: Cultural Studies.

Faculty #4: More on the Third World, gender.

Faculty #1: But the faculty will continue to drive the change. Encouragement can come from the administration, but not the decision. What's good is that they encourage, foster change.

The discussion exemplifies other discussions held at Cutting Edge. One of the interesting points in the discussion is the perceptions of the faculty about their institution. Perhaps they are not unlike faculty at other institutions. For example, it is conceivable that speaker #3 would go to a women's studies dinner if she were at another institution even though she says she would not. Speaker #2 has found alienated faculty elsewhere, but certainly other faculty work at institutions—where they are not alienated with a radically different curricular structure—Christian University comes to mind. And surely speaker #1's comment about the administration fostering change could be said at many other campuses.

Yet the faculty at Cutting Edge speak proudly, as if they are unique—in part because they are—but also because the culture of the institution provides an identity exemplified by the mission and enacted through the curriculum. Curricular decisions do not occur only because the institution seeks to adapt to a market or because someone came up with a bright idea, but because the curricular concept in some way relates to what the organizational participants perceive their institution to be.

The curriculum relates to virtually all other aspects of the organization. Research, academic management, and faculty workload all relate back to how the participants conceive of the curriculum. At Classics College faculty and student relationships are emphasized by way of teaching the curriculum; research and academic management are played down. At Working-Class State College academic management is essential, given the demands of the state, and faculty workload must be crystal-clear because of a collective bargaining agreement, which in turn structures the way people think about the curriculum.

Discussions revolve around how curricular changes will affect "what we are"; in large part "what we are" is defined not only by the curriculum, but also by how the institution achieves curricular decisions. The natural science dean at Cutting Edge speaks of her school by saying:

We were set up as a large Italian, Jewish family—lots of good fights, shouting. Some people got tired of the yelling, and now there is a toning down. We try to operate by collective decision making. I like the idea. Coming to a quick vote short-changes the discussion and doesn't help us figure out who we are, what we should be doing. It is time-consuming, however.

At Cutting Edge College and at Entrepreneurial College the curriculum evolves and continually changes as faculty interests change and new people enter. To all intents and purposes, curricular long-range planning at both institutions does not exist. "My time horizon is about a week," admits one individual at Cutting Edge. The difference between the two institutions concerns how they both interpret their mission. Both institutions have radically different conceptions of knowledge. However, both Cutting Edge and Entrepreneurial stand in sharp contrast to Working Class State where a curricular decision-making process appears static.

I should not overdramatize the differences in the academic decision making of the institutions. To claim that Working Class State never changes would be false. For example, a new management program has just been approved, which is evidence of a curricular change. However, the difficulties of implementing the program are apparent from the frustration of the architect of the program as he describes the process he went through to engineer the initiative: "You have to have perseverance, take heart, and generate support from everybody. I didn't get release time to devise this—this is all extra—and I now advise all the new students in the program—106." Whatever the impediments to change, a new program has appeared that has adapted to a market.

Similarly, it would be misleading to say that Cutting Edge remakes its curriculum every year, or that it does not see the need for a more systematic curricular decision-making process. A school dean comments, "I horse-trade a lot. I tell someone if they co-teach a basic class this year, then next year they can teach new courses." Another individual adds, "I think we are all beginning to realize that we need to understand our programmatic needs a bit better over a longer time frame." Entrepreneurial also has a relatively stable curriculum from year to year. Because of its decentralized process, however, additions to the curriculum are easy to implement, and occur quite often. Thus, both institutions do change their curricula, and the change is in keeping with their institutional missions.

The contrast between Working Class State's and Cutting Edge's curricular decision-making processes is quite stark. We find yet another distinctive manner of decision making with Classics' attempt at curricular revision. "Right now curricular change isn't done," notes one professor in the autumn. "There used to be a sense of shared understanding, and the faculty decided things as a group at the faculty meeting," says another. "If you can believe this," states a third, "faculty meetings used to be looked forward to. Everyone went. The debates, the argument, the devotion to intellectual discussion were superb. Now, no one goes. We all find better things to do." It appears that the younger faculty feel as if changes are needed in the curriculum but that the vehicle for creating change does not exist. The senior faculty feel that the college is drifting away from its original precepts and the vehicle that once existed—the faculty meeting—needs new life.

Thus, although both sets of faculty disagree about the direction of Classics, they see that the problem is a structural one. Changes in the constitution are proposed and debated. "There are no mechanisms for solving problems," says a newly tenured professor. "We have a committee that talks about the curriculum and it's a joke," sighs an older professor. "I've created ad hoc curricular committees. They've made reports and they've gone nowhere," says the president.

Between my visits in the fall and the spring the faculty have voted on revamping the constitution; the new proposals caused relatively large structural changes for curricular decision making. "I'm hopeful the new structure will get us out of the doldrums," comments one professor in the spring. Other faculty also speak optimistically that now that they have a new decision-making vehicle they will be able to take the curriculum in new directions.

Several questions arise. The four institutions mentioned here, and all colleges in general, have a variety of curricular committees. The faculty advisory council, the educational policy committee, the curricular affairs committee, and a cavalcade of acronyms exist as policy-making bodies. Some committees work well and some do not. Is it the structure that is at fault when curricular initiatives fail?

With regard to Classics College, my point is not that the new structure will obstruct change. The change may well come about because faculty perceive that they have a new structure that works, rather than the structure itself being the formula for success. It is also possible that the new structure will have little effect. A structure cannot decide what curricular direction a college should take. Many would see the structure at Cutting Edge College as something devised by an academfic Rube Goldberg—a cumbersome contraption. Yet the decision-making apparatus apparently works because it is another reflection of the culture of the institution. If an observer only looked at the organizational chart for decision making at Working Class State he or she might think WCSC has a streamlined vehicle for curricular decision making, but apparently the structure does not help them understand what changes are needed. At Entrepreneurial College the organizational chart seems to make sense, but any observer soon finds out that curricular direction or "vision" does not come from any collegewide committees. Over the years the college has experimented with a variety of different structures and committees, and all attempts at collegewide change have failed. Change takes place through individual initiatives.

I am not saying that decision-making structures are inconsequential or that they are entirely symbolic. As new requirements occur, or new programs and personnel are added or old programs change, new structures may be necessary and helpful. Particular decision-making structures suit one administrative team's style and not another's. The context in which an institution finds itself may necessitate different forums for reaching decisions. However, as we have seen in these four institutions, structures reflect the institution's culture; they are not independent of it.

As we conclude the second part of this book, a brief review is in order. We have deliberated over two key words that concern the culture of an academic institution—mission and curriculum. The mission and the curriculum have been discussed from the perspective of seven institutions. Women's College is engaged in a quite serious—sometimes acrimonious—debate about what it means to be a single-sex institution. Testimony State College is a public institution that has a distinctive mode of teaching—"seminaring"—which creates a unique bonding and culture among the participants. Cutting Edge College eschews disciplines and fosters interdisciplinary learning. Entrepreneurial College allows faculty to create a wide array of curricular programs and approaches to learning. A recent tenure denial has created confusion on the part of new faculty about the mission of the institution; attempts at collegewide change have rarely succeeded. Working Class State College is undergoing the possibility of curricular change in a community beset by unemployment. Classics College teaches the curricular canon and the faculty assume that one can attempt to master disciplinary knowledge. Finally, Christian University bases its curriculum on the teaching of the church. Clearly, each institution has a quite different way of perceiving its mission and enacting it by way of the curriculum.

The purpose of Part II has been to highlight and contrast different people's experiences and reflections of their institutions. There have been no heroes or villains. There have been no grand gestures and symbols of academic life to come to terms with an institution's mission or curricular structure. Instead, we have seen how people—administrators, faculty, parents, and students—experience and talk about their institution on a daily level.

The cultural life of an institution has been portrayed as a pastiche of competing knowledge and practices. And the pastiche is not always mellifluous, as witness the comment at Cutting Edge: "We were set up as a large Italian, Jewish family—lots of good fights, shouting." Further, the participants neither uniformly interpret the mission nor the curriculum. Some faculty at Classics question whether they should still teach the canon, as do some faculty at Christian. Even though both faculty have different conceptions of what the canon *is,* groups currently question what it *should* be. At Entrepreneurial, people appear to have given up any hope of reaching consensus about what the curriculum should be, and instead create individual programs. Individuals at Testimony bring their own interpretations to the institution and help the institution revise its conception of itself; and at Women's the debate and discord is out in the open.

By investigating the day-to-day experiences of different participants, I am trying to develop a sensitivity to the cultural aspects of the organization. Once we understand how the operations and perceptions of culture work in an organization, once we accept that an institution's mission is more than a tool for effectiveness, once we comprehend how the curriculum is more than a device for enabling students to become marketable or enriched by static knowledge, we will be able critically to examine the organizational formations that have constrained democratic action by not allowing us to imagine alternative ways of conceptualizing our ideological status.

Giroux notes, "Human beings not only make history, but they also make the constraints; and needless to say, they also unmake them. It needs to be remembered that power is both an enabling as well as a constraining force" (1983, p. 38). A study of the critical words of a postsecondary organization's culture has enabled the reader to see how organizational participants have made their history and their constraints. Part II provided the curricular topography of the institutions, and we have traversed several different curricular routes. But we must go further.

Part III directs the reader's attention to the voices at these institutions and to the faculty and administrators. We consider more systematically the enabling and constraining forces of power. Other voices also will be heard, principally those of the students. The culture of these same seven institutions is viewed from a different perspective. Rather than look at how participants give meaning to the topography of the institution, we will consider the participants themselves and hear their voices borne along the landscapes of their institutions. How are the actors liberated or constrained by the powers behind the ideologies? What do they do, or fail to do, with their own power?

III
Voices

The purpose of education, finally, is to create in a person the ability to look at the world for himself, to make his own decisions, to say to himself this is black or this is white, to decide for himself whether there is a God in heaven or not. To ask questions of the universe, and then learn to live with those questions, is the way he achieves his own identity. But no society is really anxious to have that kind of person around. What societies really, ideally, want is a citizenry which will simply obey the rules of society. If a society succeeds in this, that society is about to perish. The obligation of anyone who thinks of himself as responsible is to examine society and try to change it and to fight it—at no matter what risk. This is the only hope society has. This is the way societies change.

James Baldwin
A Talk to Teachers

5

The Languages of Faculty Cultures

This chapter examines the many languages of faculty discourse. Each of the different languages affects faculty attitudes about the curriculum. These languages are considered through the multiple lenses of faculty culture. Each culture, each different territory the faculty traverse, necessitates a different language. We will also examine the faculty role in the curricular decision-making process and the multiple faculty cultures that influence the process. Attention will also be given to how faculty perceive their relationship with the primary receivers of the curriculum—the students.

FACULTY CULTURES AND THEIR RELATIONSHIP TO THE CURRICULUM

It is a late afternoon at Testimony State College. We sit in the faculty lounge and it is quiet. This faculty member has taught at Testimony for about a decade. We have spoken about the intellectual concerns he has as a scholar and the pedagogic dilemmas in which he finds himself. Asked about the overall curriculum at Testimony and its purpose for students, he pauses, looks at the carpet, and reflects for a moment. Then, he looks up at me and says:

We need to understand both the agencies and objects of power. I don't concern myself much with the students, except to the extent that the psychiatrist is concerned with the patient. I want something to occur in our encounter. I want students to find out how tough it is to gain knowledge, what a discipline means. I want them to discover the questions a discipline can't answer. If a student develops a sense of limitations, then I've succeeded.

Later on in the discussion he adds:

If you want to change the curriculum, then change the way the faculty deal with one another. That's partially the answer to how to change the curriculum. It must also be interdisciplinary. See, it has a lot to do with the structure in which you find yourself. It is inextricably and unknowingly bound to structures of power which we can only partly understand.

Needless to say, the metaphors and language this individual uses are quite different from those that faculty on other campuses use when they speak about the curriculum and their role in shaping it. This individual does not think of providing students with the answers, but instead he proffers questions that have no answers. Although many other faculty think of the student/faculty relationship in terms of psychology, most other individuals use the language of human growth and development instead of a focus on the language that takes place during the encounter.

What is compelling about the way the individual speaks is that it reflects the culture in which he is embedded. Although faculty at most other institutions do not speak in the manner he does, faculty at Testimony do. The institutional language is quite similar for all faculty. For example, another individual at Testimony State defines a successful faculty member by saying, "It's someone who is really interested in teaching, in forcing students to go beyond the narrow confines of the discipline. It's being interested in broad academic matters and not just being a typical faculty member holed up in your office writing articles." An administrator comments that a faculty leader is "someone who understands the faculty relationship here."

Contradictions also arise. No culture is monolithic. One faculty member confides what is "really" going on:

I'll tell you what it's really like here. One-third of the faculty work terrifically hard, one third—and I'm in this category—work hard, like at other institutions. And the other third are on leisure time. They'll tell you they're busy, but it's bullshit. If you were here on a Friday you'd see a lot less people around. Testimony's challenge is to keep people motivated and not to burn out.

Another faculty member appears disappointed when asked if some faculty are on "leisure time" but says, "I suppose so. But you shouldn't try to paint Testimony as some kind of academic utopia. We have the same struggles as elsewhere, just different interpretations." Later in the conversation the individual elaborates by saying that Testimony is not an island unto itself. Faculty come from other institutions, have private lives with their own inherent pressures and struggles, and are initially socialized in graduate school just like faculty at other institutions. The individual shrugs and says, "We're swimming against the tide, and we're doing a good job of it too. Testimony has an inbredness that we try to foster, nurture. Are we perfect? No. But we're constantly working at building our own institution."

The point is that the manner in which faculty come to terms with their own lives and working relationship at an institution affects how the curriculum is conceived, changed, and carried out. To think of the curriculum in this fashion offers a different perspective on curricular change than to take a more rational approach to understanding curricular decision making and the role of different constituencies in the process. Whereas a rational analysis might take into account specific components of a curriculum as if it were a a recipe, the critical perspective allows us to consider how the structure and content of the curriculum are, to a large degree, determined by the cultural processes within which faculty interact. Necessarily, these processes hold contradictions: some faculty work hard and others do not. The unearthing of these contradictions and the ability to unmask the assumptions and practices of daily life form a central task of a critical understanding of organizational culture and the curriculum.

Clark notes, "There are ideational elements in complex organizations that do not lie outside of matters of governance but rather exist as basic sentiments that help determine the structures of governance and how they work" (1971, p. 499). If I were to make the same comment about the curriculum, then the bonding mechanisms for the faculty become centrally important. We do not generally see how faculty help define and are defined by the culture of the organization; in turn, curricular affairs become defined in terms of the culture of the organization. The question then turns on how faculty perceive their lives in the organization. Clark (1987) and Kuh and Whitt (1988) have noted how faculty operate in four interdependent cultures that influence a faculty's beliefs and attitudes: (1) the culture of the institution, (2) the culture of the national system of higher education, (3) the culture of the academic profession, and (4) the culture of the discipline. The culture of the discipline refers to assumptions about knowledge, what it means to be a member of a knowledge profession, and the relationship between society and knowledge. In this light, some faculty members will have more in common with those in their discipline than they do with those outside it, even if they work together on a daily basis. The culture of the academic profession concerns those elements that all faculty have in common, such as a concern for academic freedom. The culture of the profession transcends disciplines and institutions. The culture of the national system of higher education refers to how faculty, knowledge, and the system of higher education are intertwined and shaped by the nation's goals and objectives. The culture of the institution is both an independent stimulus for shaping faculty behaviors and the main locale where faculty enact all four of the interdependent cultures. Each of these cultures is a different layer of meaning that is in constant motion and change so that a faculty member quite often has different, even contradictory, stimuli requiring his or her attention that frames present possibilities.

An example from Cutting Edge College will highlight the changing mores of faculty and culture. The culture of the discipline has been displaced and the culture of the institution has assumed prominence. A good case can be made that the primary cultural determinants are those of the institution and the discipline, and for the vast majority of faculty in American institutions the strongest ties lie with the institutional culture.

The academic vice president notes, "You don't just want people to always internalize. You want people to get out, to have networks so that we're not too inbred. Their ideas affect how the curriculum will turn out." A faculty member hears the dean's comment and follows it up. "Don't interpret this to mean engaging in disciplinary professional associations. At least half of the faculty attend meetings of interdisciplinary groups (Latin American Studies Associations, Black Studies,

Teaching Science)." Another individual comments, "Most likely you're not going to make it professionally here. It's hard to document all that we do. The work situation, teaching, is so demanding. It's a very different place." A fourth individual speaks of her life and the demands placed on it:

The ethos is to *kvetch* a lot. We're soldiers, people who invest their whole lives in this place and we like to complain. When the semester is on you don't have a day off, you can't control your time, and when the semester is over everybody's face is dragging. There's not a lot of graciousness here, but the payoff is when you ride home on the bus and you hear a kid say to another, "I'm sorry the course is over. I learned so much. . . . "

Each of these people highlight the cultures in which the faculty are situated. Self-inference and subjectivity are involved with what each person says. Yet every comment is framed by the cultures of faculty life. Because of the intensity of the institutional culture it appears that faculty affiliation with the discipline is not so high. Interestingly, the administrator notes that the lack of a disciplinary affiliation can be a problem if the faculty begins to feed on itself for ideas, rather than also look outside. Another individual points out, however, that even when people attend conferences they generally eschew disciplinary formats. From a cultural perspective, people also speak of rewards by way of the institution rather than the discipline or profession. A faculty member at a research university might say that "the payoff" is gaining a grant, or being elected to a particular office in an association. At Cutting Edge the reward comes from teaching via the curriculum.

At Classics College the institutional culture reflects the disciplines. Classics is an interesting example because even though teaching is critically important, the faculty's relationship to their discipline resembles the relationship of a faculty of a research university to the discipline. We expect research faculty to be closely affiliated to the discipline; their socialization, reward structure, and often the major portion of time and commitment is with the discipline. The same cannot be said for a teaching faculty. Although faculty may initially be socialized to the discipline as graduate students, their professional careers are in teaching. Classics' socialization, time, commitment, and reward structure all point toward teaching as the essential task. Yet we recall the biochemist from the previous chapter who rejected the idea of inter-disciplinary work because he had so much to keep up on in his own area. As for other individuals on the Classics campus: The president notes, "Departments are too strong. People's interests lie in the de-partments, in their specialty areas." A faculty member comments, "The place has been governed by a powerful educational ideology that is tied to changes in the fields." A third person concurs: "I'm constantly reading in my area. I can't imagine trying to work across disciplines when there is so much happening in my own discipline." Again, con-tradictions also arise. A member of the psychology department is ag-grieved that the natural sciences hold psychology in disdain and will not be more collaborative. A new member of the English department expresses amazement that faculty do not talk more across disciplines.

The picture arises of an institution where the faculty culture of the institution mirrors the disciplinary culture. Yet at the same time, com-ments about the reward structure at Classics are reminiscent of Cutting Edge. "Teaching, teaching, teaching, and then maybe scholarship and good citizenship is what it takes here," comments a young professor at Classics. "The interaction with the students is invigorating, what makes it all worthwhile," says another.

A department chair at Classics notes how curricular planning is de-centralized:

Departmental structure has increased, local attention to curricular matters has become more important. I've never seen the faculty as a whole operate in any curricular planning way. Decisions are made on the basis of local needs and concerns and the availability of resources. I'm all for interdisciplinary kinds of things but it can't work here. We have our own unique structure and the department runs the show.

The faculty of Women's College has a third cultural formation. Cut-ting Edge and Classics are examples of where a faculty culture of the institution and the discipline have been quite strong, yet the reward structures are both oriented toward similar outcomes—teaching and learning. Women's College is split.

Those faculty who identify the mission of the institution as one in which a women-centered curriculum ought to be addressed are trying to create an allegiance to the institution much as Cutting Edge has done. "The battle," says one professor, "is to incorporate scholarship on women, education about women. That's where we should devote our time, teaching our students about women's education.'' Faculty who adhere to this perspective are more likely to declare fidelity to other scholars across disciplines within the institution, than to seek disciplinary rewards outside of the college. Like the faculty at Cutting Edge, Women's faculty of this persuasion may also seek compatriots outside of the institution. However, socialization concerns understanding what the institution is attempting to do, and the reward structure is geared toward the institution rather than the professions.

On the other hand, a faculty member who believes quite strongly in an institutional orientation toward the disciplines comments, ''I don't believe a discipline is an historical accident. The person who is productive here gives little to the college. The discipline is essential. People use commitment to the college as a substitute for being good in the discipline.'' A second person echoes similar sentiments when speaking about what a new dean should attempt to do. ''Respect the autonomy of the departments. What a departmental structure should be is a replication of the discipline. I want departments to tell us what should be done and not some politically minded group that advocates for a particular point of view.''

Clearly, the norms for these individuals are geared toward the discipline. The reward structure, unlike that of Classics and Cutting Edge, appears to be located in the discipline. One individual even comments negatively about commitment to the institution, implying that those who cannot succeed in the discipline become committed to the institution. Once again, the curriculum becomes a cultural clash between two groups of faculty oriented toward different cultures. The institution is both a subculture and the main arena for playing out the disagreements. The curriculum takes on added significance not just as a pedagogic tool for inculcating students with particular values, but as the raison d'etre of the college.

Weis notes, ''Faculty appear to contribute to institutional outcomes in unanticipated ways by virtue of the form their culture(s) take—a form that represents a set of accommodations to their own lived realities'' (1985, p. 572). Elaborating on that theme, I am suggesting that institutional culture is not simply imposed on individuals; rather, the interactions of different faculty cultures plays an important role in determining the culture of the organization and the form the curriculum ultimately takes within the institution. The possibilities for action, and the inability to perceive of solutions, derive from the different strata of meaning that intersect on the surfaces of faculty life. Individuals have more power and responsibility than they sometimes think because of different cultural formations that have taken place on a campus.

In general, previous investigations of the curriculum have not thought about how the curriculum-change process is linked to the cultural makeup of the faculty or the overriding ideologies implicit at the cultural level. The point is not that one can do away with one cultural form or another or, necessarily, that one cultural formation is wrong and another right. The first task is to understand how these cultures interact with one another, and how the interactions hinder or hasten each individual's ability to comprehend the cultural web in which we are all enmeshed. Once we understand how cultures interact, and our relationship in the web, we can devise strategies that seek to embolden and empower all participants.

Cutting Edge, Classics, and Women's College have provided examples of faculty disciplinary and institutional cultures. A discussion of the two public institutions will shed light on the culture of the profession and the culture of the national system of higher education. Working Class State College is a member of a state system, and the faculty have a collective bargaining agreement. Both of these facts help structure the way faculty think about and function in their jobs. "The rules are very clear," states the union president, "about how we go about deciding changes in the curriculum." "I want to have a significant impact on the curriculum, so I joined the union," comments a new professor. A new administrator observes, "I take curricular change as part of a dialogue, and the union is used to a 'take-it-or-leave-it' attitude. That's new for them. The mind-set has been different for them professionally."

A union and the rules of a union contract clearly are a cultural component neither of Working Class State nor of the discipline. Instead, collective bargaining is a component of the culture of the profession. Collective bargaining cuts across disciplines and institutions, although we might see it as a subculture within a culture. Not all members of the academic profession belong to a union; neither do all members of the discipline of anthropology belong to the American Anthropological Association. Yet at some institutions people think of themselves as faculty members belonging to a profession that is tied together by a union affiliation.

At Working Class State the culture of the profession impacts upon the curriculum. For example, the previous chapter discussed the new management program instituted at the college and the difficulties the innovator of the program had in bringing about the change. He comments about the union, "It offers protection and good salaries, but it's also an impediment to curricular change. We don't offer evening or weekend classes or extend the geographic boundaries of where we can teach because the union is against it." A nonunion faculty member states, "It bothers me being told I can't teach this or that. Politically, you pay real dues if you don't join. I've got lots of ideas that I can't implement."

The insight to be gained from these comments is not that collective bargaining or unionization on a campus is necessarily an impediment to change. Other instances can be found where collective bargaining appears as a *stimulus* for change (Chaffee & Tierney, 1988). Even at Working Class State the academic vice president states, "I don't have a problem with the union; I think it clarifies everyone's roles and responsibilities." The next step, then, is to observe how a professional component of culture such as collective bargaining affects other faculty cultures and the curriculum.

In the previous chapter the participants at Working Class State spoke about the mission of the institution in terms of jobs. Here is a similar response: "When a kid finishes, he'll find a good job that he wouldn't have gotten if he hadn't come here. A college education—computers, teaching, business administration—that kind of thing prepares students for the work world." Certainly, such sentiments can be found on countless campuses throughout America, and especially at public institutions. The sentiments come from the historical and current context of the culture of the national system of higher education and from the mass media, the arbiters of popular culture. The citizenry started public institutions to provide training for jobs. From this perspective, an institutional mission is not a free-floating object that the participants are capable of creating each year; rather, the cultural weight of the overall system of higher education "expects" particular institutions to conduct particular kinds of activities. In turn, different expectations will be held of the faculty and the curriculum. Institutions that must be responsive to the public are most influenced by the national system.

As was noted in the previous chapter, we must not overlook the relationship of class to institutional mission and type. The context in which students, faculty, and community operate is critical to understanding the relationship of the curriculum to democracy and empowerment. Obviously, Working Class State serves the people of the name I have given the college—the working class. By educating for jobs, the college faculty is reinforcing the ethos of the parents of students. "We knew our boy would get a job when he's done here," comments one father. The boy's mother adds, "His brother graduated and he's doing well, he's got a job." Working Class State has a higher proportion of working-class students attending the college than any other institution under study. The question is how faculty at Working Class State can provide gainful employment to its students while at the same time exposing the invisible structures of the curriculum and the kinds of knowledge produced in the classroom so that students understand and come to terms with the contexts in which they are embedded.

Testimony State College presents an interesting example of faculty interpreting an alternative version of the national system's culture. Rather than seek to provide jobs for students, the participants speak in a different manner about what goals they wish to fulfill. One longtime member says, "If you want to understand us, look at what the student government spends its money on. They spend it on aiding students of color, helping lesbians and gays, the environment. There is a social justice orientation here." Others echo the individual's comment. "Sure we want jobs, but the students want more than just that," says one. Most tellingly, another individual states, "I wouldn't be here if I was supposed to be concerned about job placement." Again, it is important to point out that the students of Testimony generally come from a higher socioeconomic class than at WCSC. Middle- and upper middle-class students who enter college with the expectation that they will exit with good employment possibilities are not so concerned about jobs as are working-class students. The struggle to enlighten students to the conditions in which they find themselves is still evident; but the context of the student body is radically different. Of consequence, the strategies to empower students will differ between Working Class State and Testimony.

At the start of this chapter a faculty member stated why he was at Testimony—not to help students find the right answers, and hence, jobs, but rather to help students find the right *questions*. As with Classics College, where the faculty's disciplinary culture and institutional culture blend, we see at Testimony State College the mixing of institutional culture and the culture of the national system.

Testimony State is perhaps the best example of the faculty's ability to create their reality within the parameters of their organization. The interpretation the faculty give to their purpose and how curricula are enacted is an active indicator that highlights another cultural aspect of the national system. The institution rejects the notion that education implies job training, and struggles to implement ideas concerning empowerment and democracy. The faculty's rejection of disciplinary grounds works in opposition to the cultural restrictions of the discipline. Consequently, we have participants working in an institutional culture that is rooted, in the words of Giroux, "in a fundamental belief in the possibility of public life and the development of forms of solidarity that allow people to reflect and organize in order to criticize and constrain the power of the state" (1987, p. 105).

One final example of the national system's culture concerns Christian University. As a nation that supports freedom of religion, the culture of the national system allows religious institutions to function without interference from the state except in matters of discrimination. As public institutions are part of the national system, so are religious institutions. However, today the participants at Christian University find little understanding from a culture of the national system, and they leave most of the active interpretation up to the institution. What it means to be a religious institution is no longer as clear as it once was. "I want us to be a first-class Christian university," mentions one individual, "but I don't know what that means." "Do we evangelize in the classroom or do we talk about business ethics and morals?" queries a business professor. "If you walk around here and see what's posted on trees, in the cafeteria, and everywhere, you really begin to wonder what being a Christian college means," adds one individual. His point is that the advertisements for concerts, movies, parties, and the like appear to homogenize Christian's culture with other mainstream institutions.

The culture of the institution at Christian University now competes with the discipline as younger faculty arrive whose interests in research parallel more closely those of mainstream faculty. Again, the curriculum is the principal turf on which faculty enact their changes. Different cadres of people try to incorporate their vision of a religious institution in the canon of the curriculum. A young humanities professor adds:

I know that the way we see things is different. But how we come together as a faculty and define what's what is anyone's guess. I coould teach at the [public] university in town. They offered me a job. I stayed here because we have a better chance of defining ourselves. I'm not just a humanities professor. I'm a Christian humanities professor at an institution that claims our faith defines what we do.

Given the different cultures of the faculty, we now need to look more closely at how these curricular changes come about, and the degree of faculty involvement.

THE CULTURE OF DECISION MAKING

It is 7:30 A.M. and six students await my arrival in a private dining room next to the cafeteria. Coffee, juice, rolls, cereal, and fruit are set on the table. After a quick introduction and a joke or two about how we all stumbled out of bed to get here and none of us is yet awake, I ask students for their thoughts and experiences about the curriculum and life at Entrepreneurial College.

Several of the students sit on the curriculum committee, and discussion begins immediately about their role on the committee. One student offers, "I don't feel our opinion is valued." "The basic relationship between students and faculty is that we listen and they talk. They talk about grand schemes," relates a second student. Another individual observes, "Surprisingly, they don't take into account what students want. They're not responsive to the consumer. I don't see the committee as a real vehicle for communication." The discussion continues in this vein for five more minutes until a student turns to an additional concern: "Some guy wants to do something that he thinks is interesting, but how does he know?" The others nod their heads in agreement as the student continues, "How do they know what we think? They never come and talk with us. We want to extend the classroom out into the dorm, but faculty don't want to interact."

Another student raises her voice and says, "We invite professors, but they don't show up." The student sitting nearest to me continues, "Basically, the faculty have a very condescending viewpoint. They think they know what we need, so they think up courses and majors. Faculty need to know us more, rather than just think we need to know more." A tall student at the other end of the table interrupts: "They think we're apathetic. And we are. Students don't get involved on committees. It's hard to get people excited here. Apathy results when you don't feel you have any impact on power. Empowerment. We don't have any voice."

At Christian University I sit in on an ad hoc faculty meeting about the curriculum. A dean chairs a meeting of about a dozen faculty. The group has reached the point where they are ready to suggest names to appoint to a committee that will attempt to overhaul the curriculum. Different professors' names are put forward and debated. The list grows and the dean is about to close off any more suggestions. The following short discussion takes place:

Professor #1: I hope we don't forget to have a student on this.

Dean: Oh yes, I forgot! Good idea.

Professor #2: I hope we get a good one. We should get someone who knows something, perhaps a senior or junior.

Dean: I'll talk with the Dean of Students for a suggestion.

Professor #1: It's important to get a student. They should have a voice in this.

Earlier in the day a student at Christian talks to me about student participation in meetings. He says, "They don't want us to participate, so why try? I get nervous sitting in a room with all those faculty. Who's going to listen to me? A student on a faculty committee is just a token to make them feel good." Students on other campuses make similar comments about their voice in curricular decision making. By and large they feel left out of the decision-making process even though they often have nominal representation on committees. The lack of student voice in decision making only adds to the confusion students already have about the curriculum. As one student on the Entrepreneurial campus says, "I still don't understand how everything fits. We never pause and reflect here. There's no putting it all together, no grand picture." Another student comments, "Any sort of growing I do occurs in classes, rather than the whole thing. I know myself better. It comes in spurts though. There's no vision. We don't know where we want to go. You'd think that would be the point of a curriculum committee—deciding where we want to go.''

Anyone who has served on a curriculum committee may rightly question whether a curriculum committee ever provides "vision." At Classics College a student confides that she is a "faculty watcher." She comments about how she watches faculty work on committees:

Students don't speak at faculty meetings. You have to be invited and I've been hushed at meetings for attempting to say something. They're really entertaining meetings, though. Faculty try to talk. They're perfectly able, smart. Yet they can't tie their shoes! They can never make decisions and when they do, it has nothing to do with anything.

At Entrepreneurial a young professor watches a faculty meeting and is mystified. "This was an emotional meeting. Lots of arguing, impassioned speeches. But what we were supposed to vote on was something that was already in the faculty handbook. They weren't trying to change it. It was as if we were voting to affirm that the sky is blue. Incredible!''

An example of a curriculum committee meeting at Women's College will highlight the confusion the student and faculty member feel. This committee meets monthly at 4:00 P.M. and is composed of the dean of the faculty, the associate dean, and nine faculty members from various departments. They sit in a paneled meeting room off the dean's office. Ornate, framed pictures are on the walls. Chocolate-chip cookies sit in little dishes on the table and coffee is available. The wooden table is large and rectangular. Everyone sits in straight-backed chairs and confers in small groups before the meeting is called to order.

The committee members spend the first 15 minutes talking about changes of the minutes from last month's meeting and then they approve them. They have an agenda and packet of materials for this meeting in front of them. The first item concerns a discussion about planning for an open faculty meeting. The second item concerns a questionnaire.

An hour's discussion ensues about the faculty meeting and the questionnaire. People want to know whether the questionnaire will be for information purposes or assessment purposes. "We are just in the information-gathering stages,'' states the questionnaire's chief advocate. "For the questionnaire and follow-up meeting to be useful,'' comments one professor dubiously, "it needs to be made clear that we are gathering information, as opposed to deciding what the answers ought to be." "It will help us plan a freshmen experience," explains someone else. "But we can't sit here as a committee telling departments what to do," says another.

The committee continues talking and decides to split up the questionnaire among themselves, work on it, and get back together again. They discuss another agenda item and then receive reports from representatives of other committees. The report from the Administrative Board takes up about 20 minutes of the committee's time. The representative from the Board points out a problem. The committee spends over 15 minutes discussing an Emergency Medical Treatment (EMT) course that has been offered through "Special Studies." The faculty member reports that the instructor is unqualified. The speaker seems outraged that the EMT teacher has been able to "get by" offering the course:

He doesn't have the credentials. It's almost fraud the way he has arranged to teach this course. I think we should send a memo quite clearly stating that the experimental status of this course is over. If another department wants to propose offering this course then they should do so through the regular procedure.

They turn to a few more subcommittee reports until a school bell rings, apparently indicating that the time for the meeting has ended. They gather up their papers and leave.

In interviews after the meeting in the fall and again in the spring I speak with different members of the committee. An impressive number of perceptions arise about the meeting and its outcomes. After the questionnaire has been sent and the meeting has been held, the architect of the meeting comments, "It was successful! We've decided to have a series of faculty workshops next year that will help us focus on some of the problems we located in the questionnaire and at the meeting." Disagreement, however, comes from another informant: "We're doing what they want, which won't work. Workshops! It's such a stupid waste of time!"

One person laughs about the discussion over EMT. "Can you believe we spent time discussing that! Those kinds of things are what some people love to bring up and discuss to death. And we don't even know if the course is worthwhile or not, just that the instructor doesn't have the proper credentials." However, another person says, "Basically that's what I see as the role of the committee. To be a watchdog over the place and make sure blemishes don't occur."

Undoubtedly, anyone who has observed meetings on other campuses will have seen activities such as the one portrayed here. How are we to interpret such meetings? Certainly any sense of "vision" about the curriculum is obscured at committee meetings. Instead, what surfaces are quite different interpretations of what should be discussed at meetings, and even what happens at meetings. Some faculty want to address broader institutional issues, while other faculty are more concerned with the more microscopic curricular affairs of the college. Some individuals believe the resolution to a topic is successful, and other faculty believe the outcome is a dismal failure.

Although an observer may not find any grand "vision" discussed at such meetings, what is found are examples of how small activities such as planning a faculty forum affect ideology, power and, ultimately, the curriculum of the institution. Simply the presence of a discussion by a committee, or the realization that an all-college forum should highlight what students should learn reflects a different conception than an unquestioning acceptance that knowledge should be merely updated rather than challenged. Whether the challenge to the status quo succeeds remains to be seen; yet for any challenge to triumph, it is a truism to point out that first the parameters of the issue must be defined and debated. The curriculum committee at Women's College has begun to redefine its purpose; rather than concentrate on monitoring individual courses with the expectation that the overall curriculum needs to be rethought, the committee has begun the difficult task of thinking about how its mission and curriculum relate to ideology and power.

Another point about the culture of curricular decision making is reflected in two faculty comments on different campuses. On Women's campus a faculty member reflects about faculty life and the institution's attempts at curricular overhaul. He says, "People despair so much. No matter how much we try, there is always an air of despair, that we are never successful." On the Entrepreneurial campus, a respected faculty member of many years talks about his colleagues in other departments and the failure of the institution to overhaul its curriculum.

They're a bunch of slimy little bastards up on the hill. The tension on this campus will never go away; nothing will get done as long as that large slug of people is here. They're just rabble-rousers. Some of these guys have coffee klatches and all they do is plot against us. It's a constant battle. They just sit around and plot.

In part, Entrepreneurial's lack of success at curricular overhaul exemplifies the multiple interpretations the faculty bring to the institution, and the lack of specificity the mission provides. "I won't try anymore," states a music professor. "I put in my time in trying to come up with a general education component, and nothing happened." Another individual comments, "We make attempts at change—some of them are very serious attempts, too. But we always fail." A dean concludes, "We have a very good curriculum. Students learn here. But I think most people have given up the expectation that we will reach consensus around a common core of knowledge." One other faculty member agrees with the dean, but sighs and says, "Yet deep down, I think many of us wish we could agree, that we could find a common core."

Unlike Classics, where the faculty feel that their inability to reach agreement is a structural problem, the faculty at Entrepreneurial believe that the structure is *not* at fault. "We have very strong disagreements about the nature of knowledge," concludes a longtime professor. "At the least, we have reached a peaceful impasse where we agree to disagree." Curricular innovations rarely occur neither because the structure of the decision-making process is too cumbersome, nor because the institution lacks the necessary funds to carry out any changes, but because cadres of people operate from adumbrated ideologies that stand in sharp distinction from one another.

Faculty bring to their work experiences different cultural baggage, and as they sit on committees and deliberate over curricular change, the serious differences of opinion that stem from their own cultural backgrounds stymie change. When I say that individuals have different cultural backgrounds I do not mean only the class, racial, or sexual orientation of an individual. Although an understanding of organizational culture certainly takes into account individual backgrounds and styles, the analysis called for here is more concerned with the culture of the faculty—of the disciplines, of the profession, of the national system, and of the institution. As Clark notes, "Our exploration of the 'academic mind' . . . has shown an abundance of concerns that are not self-interest narrowly conceived" (1987, p. 140). The different languages, the different voices that faculty employ as they decide about the curriculum creates a particular form of cultural politics.

Student voices are mute because we do not know how to incorporate their voices, to listen to their words, within the discourse surrounding faculty life. As we shall see, many times administrative voices are also often discounted because administrators are placed in an oppositional category from the faculty. And faculty themselves decry one another's voices as they attempt to thwart challenges to what they see as suggestions to overthrow the accepted canons of knowledge.

But knowledge is not something "out there" lying unconnected to a faculty member's experience and sense of self. An individual is socialized to think and act a certain way; particular activities are also rewarded and other activities go unrecognized. Belief and meaning in the worth of one's work come from the day-to-day activities the faculty member carries out (Tierney, 1988). Even a minor curricular change implies a challenge to the accepted cultural order. A change in the manner in which a group decides to discuss issues inevitably reflects back on the faculty member.

Several worthwhile works have been developed that outline how innovations or curricular decisions can be facilitated (Mayhew & Ford, 1971; Hefferlin, 1969; Chickering, et al., 1977). These authors work from the assumption that organizations are rational entities, and the writers overlook the cultures of the faculty. Rather than look at the curriculum as the arena where cultural politics are played out, previous works have looked at faculty attitudes about the curriculum as problems of "turf" that can be solved by primarily rational-political means. When we use a cultural lens rather than a rational image to consider faculty behavior and curricular change, a different way of thinking about the curriculum arises, and hence, different decision-making strategies come forth.

From this perspective, the problem at Entrepreneurial College is not that disagreements arise over what a curriculum should look like; but that no one has a sense of a guiding vision—other than in the broadest of terms. The individualist logic of Entrepreneurial College allows faculty the freedom to construct their own interpretations of the curriculum. With its "realist" epistemology, Entrepreneurial does carry out what it says it will do. In short, the shared conviction of the institution is a dictum that one is free to do as he or she chooses. But it appears that individuals want more from the institution. The confusion arises when new faculty are unsure how to interpret the mission, or when older faculty feel disenfranchised.

In some respects Entrepreneurial's culture is the opposite of Working Class's—and the culture is as difficult for Entrepreneurial's participants to unmask. Whereas Working Class has a culture that gets narrowly defined by the nature of its public mandate—a public state institution for the working class—Entrepreneurial has a culture that gets broadly defined by the history and context of its own surroundings. Paradoxically, I suggest that participants at each institution have the same task; they need to interpret the inner workings of their culture and come to terms with defining what the most productive route to expanding democracy is.

In short, academe is a cultural network composed of contradictory groupings of faculty who often have only tenuous bonds either to one another, within the institution, or across institutions. Faculty speak different languages across institutions and disciplines. Clearly, the professor who calls his colleagues "slimy little bastards" has found little in common with faculty in other disciplines at Entrepreneurial. In part, his disappointment and anger stems from the rigor he feels as a scientist, and what he perceives is the academic shallowness of his colleagues in the social sciences and humanities. He continues, "The humanities used to think kids should take whatever they want; now they want to redo the curriculum to meet their agenda. They've never listened to the scientists."

The professor's sentiments will also be found at Women's College between those who want to institute a new mission, and those who want to sustain the traditional liberal arts curriculum. Similar comments erupt at Classics College where faculty disagree over the nature of the desired curriculum. However, the analysis of these differences should extend beyond merely summarizing the conflicts by political groupings—liberal vs. conservative, young vs. old, disciplinary vs. interdisciplinary, scientists vs. social scientists, and the like. I do not mean to imply that such groupings do not exist. Clearly, they do. However, as I have argued elsewhere (Tierney, 1988a), culture arises in relation to a number of internal institutional characteristics as well as factors external to the institution. The struggle is to be able to understand the characteristics and comprehend the cultural differences that exist. Rather than try to ameliorate the differences or ignore them, we must confront the differences and figure out ways to deal with them.

How might we think about the competing voices of the faculty? As Clark asks, "Beyond weakening attachment to attenuating broad principles, is there anything left, any linkage that somehow connects the many parts to the whole?" (1987, p. 141). From the perspective taken in this work, "anchoring ideologies become a crucial element" (Clark, 1987, p. 144). Depending on a faculty member's orientation, he or she will speak a different language. Some faculty are multilingual; many are not. By speaking different languages, the views they express, the paths they take, and the vistas they ultimately want to explore and reach, will differ. How do we reconcile the differences?

The problem relates back to the discussion of institutional mission and ideology. Faculty cultures are linked in critical ways to institutional outcomes. The cultures both are created by and help create the overriding ideology that permeates both the institution and the profession. Weis notes, "Faculty, by virtue of their perspectives and practice, possess the power to thwart, whether consciously or not, institutional goals" (1985, p. 573). We socialize faculty to a variety of narrow interests either in the discipline or the institution. From their specialized interests, faculty react either positively or negatively to proposals put forward at a curriculum committee.

It should be clear by now that institutional ideologies or missions do not change by decree; they are debated and fought over either implicitly or explicitly by rival factions. The parameters of the debate, those whose voices are heard and those whose voices are silent, are the first volleys of the argument. External actors such as those mentioned in Part I— Bloom, Bennett, Holland—help frame the nature of the argument to which faculty react. Internal actors most dependent on the external forces—managers in charge of administering the institution—respond by insuring that their organization is effective, or efficient, or whatever particular phrase is invoked at the time. Faculty can stymie goals or they can support them.

Another way to think about the process, however, is to see how faculty can *create* goals that reaffirm the unique nature of the educational process and their institutions. I am referring to a faculty's ability to exercise forms of intellectual and pedagogic practice that locates the curriculum directly into a cultural sphere by arguing that the curriculum represents a struggle over ideology, and necessarily, power relations. We discover then, that the discourse created at a curriculum committee meeting or a faculty member's reflection about colleagues is directly related to how the institution creates and disseminates knowledge. In so doing we should consider other key actors in the process. We will continue to hear from students about the way they see their lives and what they learn at their institutions. But it is now time to turn full attention to the academic managers of the institution—the presidents, academic vice presidents, and deans.

6

Trail Guides: Academic Administrators

A vast body of literature exists concerning administrators in higher education. Broadly, I will characterize the works in two categories. The bulk of the writing comes from organizational behavior and deals with effective management. A second smaller group of studies begins with the assumption that administrators are the cause of many of higher education's problems, and that "managers" are anathema to the higher education enterprise. Prior to listening to the voices of presidents, academic vice presidents, deans, and their critics, I will briefly discuss the literature in both categories to situate the case studies in relation to previous works.

FRAMING ADMINISTRATION

Administrators as Managers

To purport to survey the literature on both administrative and organizational behavior in a brief discussion is somewhat presumptuous. However, it is important to understand the orientation of the volume of literature that has been written about academic administration. Books such as *Managing the Academic Enterprise* (Ehrle & Bennett, 1988), *Managing the Academic Department* (Bennett, 1983), *Chairing the*

Academic Department (Tucker, 1984) and *Leadership Roles of Chief Academic Officers* (Brown, Ed., 1984) subscribe to notions that academic administrators are managers, individuals who try to manage both people and resources effectively.

Although most of the literature recognizes that differences exist between businesses and colleges and universities, the work of the postsecondary manager, in essence, is not much different from managing a business. Although academic managers must be concerned about concepts such as sharing authority with the faculty, ultimately managers operate the enterprise efficiently and effectively. For example, Gould states, "There is constant need for balance between necessary faculty authority and desirable administrative efficiency" (1964, p. 1). Mortimer and Caruso point out the demands that confront academic administrators: "the need to reallocate people and programs in response to changing student demand, the need for some institutions to get smaller, and the need for short-term retrenchment" (1984, p. 43). The work, then, of academic administrators is not so much in the development of ideas or the furthering of particular lines of inquiry, but in the manipulation of different levers to ensure that the organization functions smoothly.

Other writers have disputed whether administrators are capable of producing change. James March and his colleagues (March & Olsen, 1979; Cohen, March, & Olsen, 1972; March, 1978) have labeled highereducation organizations "organized anarchies" because they have unclear goals, fluid participation, and an unclear technology. Their general concern is to understand how administrators might be able to manage ambiguity. March and Olsen have commented, "We remain in the tradition of viewing organizational participants as problem solvers and decision makers. However, we assume that individuals find themselves in a more complex, less stable, and less understood world than that described by standard theories" (quoted in Scott, 1981, p. 272).

It is fair to say that most of the work concerning administrative theory has viewed administrators as "problem solvers and decision makers." Even newer views of organizations, such as functionalist conceptions of organizational culture, remain focused on the precept of the administrator as manager. As with March, cultural functionalists often do not focus on structural tools that the manager can use to increase efficiency; instead, culturally functional studies investigate how managers might orchestrate the symbolic side of the organization more effectively. The emphasis for cultural functionalists, however, remains on solving organizational dilemmas.

Administrators as Problems

As far back as 1918, writers criticized the supposition that higher education needed to be administered. The authors sometimes violently disagreed that colleges and universities were like businesses. These critics disdained administrators whose function was to manipulate faculty and lessen the collegial voice in decision making. Thorstein Veblen, for example, wrote in *The Higher Learning in America*, a broadside against the imposition of businesslike practices into the academic life: "It appears that the intrusion of business principles in the universities goes to weaken and retard the pursuit of learning, and therefore to defeat the ends for which a university is maintained" (1957, p. 165). In *The Goose Step*, Upton Sinclair followed a similar line of thinking. In discussing the life of a university president he wrote,

He rules the university as an absolute autocrat; he permits not the slightest interference with his will. He furiously attacks or cunningly intrigues against anyone who shows any trace of interference, nor does he rest until he has disgraced the man and driven him from the university. His "faculty council" is a farce, because it has only advisory powers, and he overrides it when he sees fit (1923, p. 40).

To Veblen, Sinclair, and other critics of higher education, academe did not need to be "managed." Instead, the academic enterprise needed to be left to the faculty to govern as a collegium where intellect and reason guided decisions, not concerns about "reallocating people and resources" or "the need for short-term retrenchment."

As with Veblen and Sinclair, in some contemporary writers' views, administrators are not merely a necessary nuisance, but a hindrance to the basic purposes of academe as the university undergoes professionalization. For example, Aronowitz states: "The academic system has increasingly adopted the corporate managerial practice of recruiting professional managers for high university positions. Even when administrators hold formal academic credentials these serve as legitimizing fig leaves for a professionalized management" (1985, p. 10). In this light, a professionalized management only serves to legitimize the rights of the dominant and to silence the voices of the minority. Elsewhere Aronowitz notes that the professionalization of management has taken authority out of the hands of the faculty and placed decision making in a hierarchical structure. He points out that in earlier times the faculty's determination of a decision such as tenure was tantamount to appointment, whereas in the present system, "a 'higher' authority in the persons of deans, provosts, and college presidents reserves the right to veto or reverse faculty decisions" (1985, p. 10).

New critics such as Aronowitz have much in common with their earlier brethren. They object to administrators primarily on two grounds. First, the new critics insist that power and authority in decision making must remain in the hands of the faculty. Second, their insistence for faculty control of decision making is the presumption that administrators will not base decisions such as tenure on the basic tenets of the university, but instead they will bring in criteria such as cost-effectiveness, faculty-student ratios, and the like. In short, the assumption is that the university is becoming—or has become—a for-profit business where concern for academic freedom, collegiality, and the intellect is lessened.

As noted in Part I, I view administrators in a different light from either the new critics or the traditionally minded organizational theorists. While I understand the concerns of the new critics, the picture they paint of administrators often has little to do with any substantive data, so that the reader ends up with a superficial picture of administrators as desperadoes who waylay faculty wagon trains traveling through perilous territories. Surely poor or ill-willed administrators exist, but from observations for this study and other research (Tierney, 1988; Chaffee & Tierney 1988) I am hard-pressed to ascertain that administrators are any better or worse than other constituencies in academe.

On the other hand, although organizational theorists have provided a wealth of data about administrators, they have neglected the study of administrative science as a moral science. In this light, researchers must do more than describe administrative behavior from an atheoretical, amoral point of view. William Foster is worth quoting at length on this point:

Administration is a *purposive* activity: it is designed to achieve the purposes of the institution. Not all institutions have similar purposes; therefore administration is *not* generic but dependent on the nature of the institution. In *educational* institutions, the function of administration is to be *educative*, while in profit-seeking institutions, the function of administration is to realize a profit (1986, p. 24).

Foster's view calls into question much of the previous work on organizational theory. Accordingly, I reject the idea of the new critics that administrators are at the least nuisances to be overcome and at the worst ill-willed bureaucrats. Instead, I will portray administrators in much the same light as faculty—as individuals enmeshed in a culture that is not always understood, and as both subjects and objects of that culture. Administrators are more like trail guides traveling over new terrain. Through their experiences and perceptions they may be able to help the institution's participants reach their destinations. Seen in this light, administrators will not speak with one voice or interpret the terrain uniformly. Rather than view administrators in a negative light or provide examples that will highlight administrators as technocratic experts, we will hear their own voices and what others say about them. In Part IV we will return to a discussion of administrators as moral educators.

PRESIDENTS

A consistent message of the seven institutions comes from the university presidents. At Entrepreneurial College the president states:

I am deeply concerned about curricular matters. From the moment of my arrival I stood up in front of students and faculty and told them to address the curriculum. I expressed disappointment that we hadn't moved further. I have some ideas about what to do, but I will not tell the faculty. It is their responsibility, their prerogative.

At Women's College the president makes a similar comment: "I can raise the issues, articulate the weaknesses, but I will not point a direction about what we should do. That's the faculty's job." At Testimony State the president says, "I think of myself as Commissioner of the Federal Trade Commission. Truth in advertising. Does our curriculum do what we say? I point out problems I see and then let the faculty do it." At Cutting Edge people speak of the president as knowledgeable about the curriculum but, "not really that interested." Presidents, then, express varying degrees of concern about the curriculum, and in general do not take key roles in the development of curricular change.

The concept of shared authority plays a large part in presidential reluctance to take on the curriculum as a key presidential issue. "You have to know who's responsible for what," comments Entrepreneurial's president, "otherwise everyone will be stepping on one another's toes." Presidents and faculty do not perceive that curricular issues are or should be presidential concerns, and when presidents wade into the fray about what curricular changes should occur, the perception is often that they are stepping on faculty "toes."

Increasingly, presidents are seen both by faculty and themselves as fund-raisers. "We have a banker president," says a longtime faculty member at Classics College. A confidant of the president at Testimony State says, "The president's always speaking about fund-raising, about how hard it is to get funds out of the legislature, wealthy individuals." A member of the curriculum committee at Women's College comments, "The president doesn't have time to think about the curriculum. You can't do everything. On the road raising funds. That's what our president does." The alumnae director of Women's concurs: "I travel with the president quite a bit. We meet alumnae, keep them informed, try to raise funds. The president speaks beautifully about our college, about what we are doing—about the curriculum, too."

The manner in which presidents speak about the faculty, and the faculty speak about presidents, highlights the different worlds each group inhabits. In the autumn on Entrepreneurial's campus, the president vividly describes the different worlds. In a large room with overstuffed chairs the president crosses his legs, puts his hand on his chin and looks out of his office window onto a magnificent, multicolored fall scene, punctuated by groves of trees. A clock ticks; otherwise the room is quiet. The president pauses for a moment and then speaks about his relationship with his faculty:

I want so badly to be a faculty member—I really do! The first impulse is to be just one of the guys. First among equals doesn't seem to work. People don't want that. I consider myself a faculty member, I still teach, but there is an unfortunate separation. You can't go home again. For example, I don't have lunch with the faculty. When I sit down with faculty in the lounge the conversation changes. I'm not one of the guys. And I ask you, is this bad?

If Entrepreneurial's president were to pose his rhetorical question to the faculty—if it is bad that he is "not one of the guys"—he would find the answer he assumes. The responses speak to the different worlds. "We really don't have a president who's one of us, a scholar president," says one elder statesman from Entrepreneurial's faculty. A colleague absorbs the comment and adds, "We have a fund-raiser, a manager. I really am not sure if we want a visionary leader, a man of letters. I don't know if we'd let someone guide us. Those days may be over. The days of the Eliots and Lowells." And a third Entrepreneurial professor states, "There's a jealous guarding of faculty turf, especially when it comes to intellectual matters. The president knows. Hands off!"

In the spring the president of Entrepreneurial elaborates on the differences he feels are necessary between faculty and president, and points out how he tries to ameliorate the differences. (We recall that between the fall and the spring three faculty have been notified they will not be granted tenure.) The president comments:

This should not be seen as a power struggle between faculty and administrators. I try to show my concern. The younger faculty have a forum I show up to, to show that I am interested in what they are doing. I want them to see—especially the younger faculty—that the president is intellectually curious about their research. I am not just a bureaucratic manager.

However, the younger faculty at Entrepreneurial do not perceive the president's attendance the way the president intends. Instead, two young women faculty converse about the president's attendance at the forum in the following manner:

Faculty #1: We developed an informal kind of a thing, a junior faculty forum.

Faculty #2: It's for junior faculty from across the college.

Faculty #1: The original purpose was to be able to present your research to your peers, to people who weren't evaluating you.

Faculty #1: To bring things that weren't in final form and get feedback.

Faculty #2: And then the president showed up! I don't know what he thought he was doing there.

Faculty #1: He just sat there.

Faculty #2: You know the president gets an impression of somebody by something like that, maybe his only impression.

Faculty #1: And this was supposed to be informal!

Thus, where a president thought he was reaching out to a constituency to demonstrate his support and interest, the constituency viewed his attendance as intrusive and threatening. The president intended his presence at a meeting to imply one symbol and the young faculty interpreted the president's attendance in a completely different manner. Given the example, one may well wonder if the gap can or *should* be bridged between faculty and administrators. Returning to Women's College and Classics College will shed some additional light on what faculty expect of a president.

The two camps of the faculty at Women's—those who believe the curriculum should reflect women's scholarship, and those who feel that the curriculum should reflect the eternal verities of Western civilization—have much to say about the president. An African American administrator criticizes the president: "The president could exert leadership over the faculty, voice misgivings that the curriculum doesn't reflect the concerns of people of color. Instead, the president's worried that the college is getting bad publicity when we speak out against racism." "I think the president should have standing dinner dates with different segments of the faculty so that everyone's position is understood not just about curriculum, but about other issues of the faculty as well," adds a leading voice of the faculty. Another tenured professor comments, "Faculty are quite strong here. I don't know what the president can do other than listen and quietly control resources, pointing things in different directions."

Given that solutions about the role of the president in curricular affairs are not forthcoming, one can understand why presidents stand aloof from the curricular process. Besides, "that's what we have academic vice presidents for," states Entrepreneurial's president.

As with Entrepreneurial's president, faculty at Classics appear uncomfortable with the presidential role. "The man has never attended a class, sat in on a discussion, in all the time he's been here. How could he have anything to say about the curriculum?" asks a senior faculty member. Another senior faculty member agrees: "The president got this idea about Asian Studies. He thought he saw a market, went out and got some money, and now it's part of our curriculum. That has been his approach to curricular innovation. We are against it."

Presumably a president should have little if any say in curricular affairs. None of the seven institutions has an activist president who concerns him- or herself about the curriculum. Some are moderately interested, and others not at all. The impression faculty create is that presidents do not understand their institutions well enough and, in general, presidents act more like managers locating markets than faculty concerned with the intellect. Even the presidents appear to hesitate about raising their voices on the intellectual turf of the faculty. The reluctance of the faculty and presidents to accept an active presidential role in curricular affairs does not necessarily stem from a presidential inability to understand faculty life. For example, the presidents of Cutting Edge, Women's, and Entrepreneurial were faculty themselves prior to becoming presidents. Entrepreneurial's president still teaches and publishes. Why, then, is there such a reluctance to listen to what a president has to say about the curriculum? Why do the presidents say so little? If given the opportunity, what might presidents say? Prior to proffering an answer I will turn to academic vice presidents and investigate their relationship to the curriculum; as one president noted above, "that's what we have academic vice presidents for."

CHIEF ACADEMIC ADMINISTRATORS

The chief academic administrators of the seven institutions make similar comments about the daily struggles they encounter on their campuses. The academic vice president (AVP) at Working Class State College speaks of the workload: "I have too many meetings and too much mail that I have to respond to. I get here at eight, eat lunch at my desk, stay until six-thirty and go home and work until nine." Entrepreneurial's AVP speaks of institutional commitments: "I probably have ten meetings a week that people expect me to attend. That's a substantial time commitment, and I'm not sure it's wisely spent."

All of the AVP's have pictures of themselves as furiously busy, and quite often, the initiatives they want to enact are met with suspicion, opposition, or boredom. For example, the academic vice president at Working Class State College has been at his job for less than six months when I meet him. He was a faculty member at another public institution that is radically different from Working Class State. He is energetic, hardworking, and has a multitude of ideas about what he wants to do. He appears to be exactly the kind of individual the institution wanted when they began their search. One individual associated with the search for a new academic vice president states:

We wanted a self-starter, a go-getter. Someone who had been at a different kind of institution and had ideas about where we should go. I look on it as a plus that we got someone who wants to shake things up a little bit and isn't just going to keep things as they are.

The same individual follows that statement by commenting on advice he would give the new academic vice president:

I'd tell him to go slow. To stay the course. Don't rock the boat. He'll find we're willing to change, but he needs to understand us before he goes off half-cocked. Just because his ideas worked somewhere else doesn't mean that they'll work here. And that's not because we're stick-in-the-muds either! I'll tell you, we've got a good faculty, but we won't just go for any new idea that floats to the surface.

What is startling about these comments is that not only are they from the same individual, but the speaker also makes the comments virtually on top of one another in the same conversation. In one breath the speaker talks about the need for "someone who wants to shake things up"; in the next, his advice to the AVP is not to "rock the boat." If individuals are this ambivalent, how is one to expect consensus among groups?

Other individuals at Working Class State provide similar comments during my fall and spring visits. In the fall one individual comments, "We want someone who will get things going. We're too sleepy, too lethargic." Again, in the fall, an additional speaker points out, "We have ways of doing things here that make good sense. I'm not anti-change but, like they say, 'If it ain't broke, don't fix it.' " In the spring one person states, "He started off too quickly in the fall, thinking he could change us overnight. He's learned, I hope!" Such comments put the AVP in something of an existential dilemma, placing him forever on shifting ground.

Unlike an institution such as Women's College, Working Class State College does not have sharply divided groups on campus. The comments cannot be divided between those who want change and those who do not. Rather, the comments offered here are representative of the entire faculty. On the one hand, the faculty want change, yet on the other hand, they will resist anyone's attempts to create change. How is the AVP at Working Class State to proceed? What trails should he attempt to walk down?

If the AVP were to observe his counterpart at Christian University he would find quite different expectations of the academic vice president.

The AVP at Christian University has worked at the institution for over ten years, and he has spent his academic life in similar kinds of institutions. Christian is in between Working Class State and Women's College with regard to faculty disagreement. Some faculty want change and others do not; the faculty camps are not so sharply divided as at Women's, yet they are more clearly drawn than at Working Class.

The faculty's comments at Christian about the AVP in general are in stark contrast to those of Working Class State. "All we get are laundry lists from him, no vision," complains one faculty member. "We have no sense of direction, no idea what kind of curriculum we should have, what we should choose to do. Instead, some of us just go our merry way, and others stagnate," points out an individual. Another person comments, "We get no sense of a three-point sermon of 'Here's where I'm going' with the curriculum. He's wise, thoughtful, but he appears to be caught up in the system."

From these comments it appears that the faculty want an AVP with "vision" who will offer insight into how the institution should change its curriculum. It is certainly plausible that if the AVP provided a "three-point sermon" of "Here's where I'm going" he might meet with forms of resistance similar to the AVP at Working Class. However, it seems the faculty want someone to provide direction; unlike Working Class's AVP, the academic vice president at Christian has a better chance of understanding the culture of the organization since he has been there for over a decade. Yet Christian's AVP is not a cartographer who maps out large landscapes of curricular change; he views the curriculum as pieces of a trail that occasionally need maintenance and always need monitoring.

Another view of an AVP who should have some understanding of the culture of the institution comes from Testimony State College. This AVP has been at the institution over five years and has had experience at similar schools. By and large, the faculty speak with one voice; they have a quite different view of what they expect from the AVP than the faculty of Christian. A faculty member who has been at the institution since the inception of the college states:

If you don't teach here you don't have credibility, and more importantly, you'll never understand this place, or the faculty. The AVP doesn't teach. He's consultative, he's a nice man, but he doesn't provide direction. We do. The

AVP thinks in terms of models he's known. The administration is almost superfluous here.

People consistently make similar comments both about the individual and the office. The faculty view the administration not so much in a we-they manner; they view the administration as a somewhat necessary appendage to the central life of the institution. What should an AVP do in a situation where the majority view is that administrative work is "superfluous"? At Testimony State the AVP acknowledges what the faculty think and states, "Grand plans, or anything like academic planning on my part won't work. I must be consultative and work quietly. Faculty must own the decision. For it to work, people cannot say 'this is the AVP's idea.' "

Cutting Edge College will provide a final example of faculty perceptions of the academic vice president's position. As opposed to viewing the role as dispensable, the faculty at Cutting Edge see the AVP as the linchpin. One person who has been at the institution for over a dozen years sums up the faculty's feelings:

When the president leaves it won't be such a big deal. We know the kind of person we need, someone who will raise money, feel comfortable dealing with the external community. No, the real fight will come when the AVP leaves. There's no one visible who I know who can do it. It will have to be an insider. We do not do well with outsiders, who don't understand us. That position is the key to keeping us the way we are.

When other Cutting Edge faculty hear a summary of the above statement they provide modifications, but they agree. "The AVP's position is not *the* key, that's too strong. But I'm sure a lot of battles will be fought over the kind of person we want," says one person. Another individual says, "It might very well be a big deal when the president leaves, but it's certain that we'll have a lot of soul-searching to do when the AVP steps down." And finally, a third individual comments, "I'm not happy that we all think the position has to be an insider. I worry about inbredness. But I think it will be an insider."

Compare the comments of the Cutting Edge faculty with those of Christian, Working Class, and Testimony State Colleges. Participants at Christian University feel that the AVP has not developed a sense of the institution and how ideology and everyday practice interact; "he is too involved with the minute activities of his office," says one individual. The Working Class State faculty apparently do not want an outsider to change things too quickly; the new AVP first has to understand "the way we do things." Faculty at Testimony State feel the AVP does not understand them—even though he has been there for over five years—because he does not teach. The Cutting Edge faculty worry that someone from the outside simply will not be able to interpret correctly the culture of the institution.

In each of the four institutions—Testimony State, Christian, Working Class State, and Cutting Edge—a different conception of the academic administrator's role and position in the culture is apparent. Participants in one institution say they want the AVP to create change, but they resist it; in a second institution they say they want direction but do not get it; in a third institution they say the AVP's position does not matter, and in a fourth institution they say the AVP is critical to the college.

What are we to make of these comments? Clearly, any rationalist blueprints for administrative action will be derailed by the decontextualized nature of the recommendations. As we listen to the participants describe their thoughts and feelings about their academic administrators, how the notion of culture circumscribes administrative authority becomes clearer. In some cases the culture will call for active academic administrators, and in other cases the culture moves the authority of the AVP away from the culture's center. Individuals in the role of AVP also exert their own interpretations and styles about what needs to be done.

Geertz comments that leaders ought to have "a deep, intimate involvement—affirming or abhorring, defensive or destructive—in the master fictions by which they order lives" (1983, p. 146). In the examples presented here, the academic administrators need to have an understanding of "the master fictions" through which faculty order their lives. Such a view locates the concept of authority within the realm of an organization's culture. In other words, an academic administrator is not defined abstractly, but as an individual whose work life is located in a particular place and draws its meaning and interpretations from different sets of relationships. It is these relationships from which academic administrators gain the authority that enables them to act. As

Wolin states, "power involves not only acting so as to effect decisive changes; it also means the capacity to receive power, to be acted upon, to change, and be changed" (quoted in Giroux, p. 28).

On one level, the AVP at Testimony State and the AVP at Cutting Edge disagree about the way they see their roles and their relationship with the faculty. At Testimony State the AVP says:

I'd like the faculty to realize the difference between policy and managerial decisions. Faculty decide policy, but once a policy decision is made, that's it. I respect faculty voice, but they expect to participate in all decisions. They are spasmodically involved, and it slows things down. I question where is the most fruitful involvement. I spend an enormous amount of time massaging things through, convincing people over and over again.

And Cutting Edge's AVP:

You have to develop constituencies and be tuned into the major constituencies of the campus. Always teach. Co-teach. Make intellectual connections. Have advisees. Chair committees. People are able to see me in roles other than the vice president. It's important for me to make other intellectual links. I try to go to all of the events. I enjoy doing it. They want someone to appreciate what they do. I try to read everything they write. It matters to people.

In one light, one individual sees himself as a manager and decision maker. He implements the policies of the faculty. Because of tangled lines of authority the AVP feels he is constantly cajoling faculty into accepting the way the administration interprets and implements the policies the faculty make. The other individual sees herself less as a manager and more as a colleague. In her eyes she has been a successful administrator because she reaches out to faculty in ways other than as a manager implementing the policies of the faculty.

The point of the examples of the AVPs at Testimony and Cutting Edge is to highlight how administrative interpretation of the fictions the faculty have created can greatly differ. Participants in a culture have quite different expectations of authority, and, conversely, participants in authoritative positions interpret their cultures in dramatically different ways. Individual nuances and interpretations will undoubtedly differ. The important point is not to assume that all administrators must act in a similar manner.

For instance, the reader could interpret the above examples as a "good" administrator and a "bad" administrator; such interpretations, however, would be misleading. The culture of Cutting Edge and the culture of Testimony State are quite *different*; the circumstances in which both individuals can act also differ. To be sure, similarities also exist. Numerous individuals at Testimony State have noted that it would help the AVP if he taught a class. Yet differences in style will not necessarily account for administrative success or failure. Listen, for example, to the comments of one faculty activist at Testimony State:

The AVP doesn't teach and that's a problem. But guess what? Quietly, he's begun to exert his own form of moral leadership. He firmly believes, for example, that we have not done a good enough job in the hiring of people of color and he's taken it on as an issue. He would not have done that a year ago, and he may not succeed. But he has a sense of mission and that's critical here.

The example points out how an AVP not only must interpret the fictions of the faculty, but that an AVP may also help create a reality, and help interpret the ideology of the institution for the faculty. And the seven institutions of this study have radically different ideological and cultural constructions. In many respects the faculties of Testimony and Cutting Edge are more alike than different; both faculties value and reward teaching. A Classics College faculty member also made a similar comment about the president—"He's never visited a class"—implying the importance of teaching. However, at Christian and Working Class the faculties have different notions of what they value. Simply stated, different trails demand different kinds of guides and interpretations. Conversely, all guides will offer unique interpretations of a trail. Yet any individual who is overcommitted and must spend hours in committee meetings will undoubtedly express unhappiness that administrative action is not smoother and more efficient. The challenge for academic administrators is to interpret the culture and to see how they may expose the underpinnings of the culture and point it, in Foster's words, "in an educative direction."

The manner in which chief academic administrators interpret their organization often percolates by way of other academic administrators such as school deans. I now briefly discuss those academic administrators who report to the AVP before concluding the chapter.

School Deans, College Deans

A faculty member at Women's College remembers:

A few years ago I took a turn as a dean. During the summer I packed up my books in boxes and as I was taking them over to the administration building, a professor who I know rather well bumped into me. I thought he was going to help me with the boxes. Instead he told me, "I just want you to know that as long as you're in that building, you're one of them, I won't be talking to you." I thought he was kidding. You know what? He wasn't! He didn't talk with me until I finished my term and moved back to my faculty office.

It is true that on some campuses, faculty who become deans are seen as "going over to the other side," as if they have acquiesced to the enemy. Again, it is not predetermined that faculty feel one way, or that a dean defines his or her authority in a particular manner. Witness the variety of interactions of the deans in the different organizations' cultures:

At Entrepreneurial College a dean comments on his first year as a dean: "I went to every department and asked every faculty member to write to me about what they think should be our priorities, and which priorities they are willing to work on. I hope it comes across that I don't have a curricular model I want to impose." At Christian University a school dean comments, "A lot of what I do is just common sense. Lots of paperwork that cleans up the process. We don't plan on a grander scale because when we direct a question to the AVP he'll respond with four hundred other questions." At Cutting Edge College a dean states, "I spend a lot of time anticipating what's going to happen. The opportunity I have is to raise issues, set the terms of discussion, and I have a certain amount of initiative. I get to propose the definitions of search committees, for example."

At Testimony State College a faculty member comments on the deans by saying, "Pegs and slots. It's not a very creative job. They find holes that need to be filled, and then they fill them. The deans get involved in everything so then they say we need more deans." At Working Class State College a new dean responds, "I'm alone. I don't have a team. I don't get to bounce ideas off anyone because I don't have any other deans."

At Entrepreneurial College a faculty member warns, "They should realize that any administrative initiative is the kiss of death. A previous dean tried something and the faculty just wouldn't go along with it.'' Another individual concurs, ''They're all alike. Deans are like widgets. They think alike and act alike. A dean's imprimatur on an institution isn't very great. A different dean would likely make the same decisions.''

Each of these comments offers different insights into the job of a dean. One dean expects guidance from the AVP, and another dean bemoans the lack of colleagues. One dean sees the job as a manager who ''cleans up the process'' and another dean views himself as first among equals. One dean feels that he accomplishes goals he sets, and another person views deans' ideas as certain to end up in the trash basket. Another dean relates in a bemused tone: ''I know I'm doing my job correctly because I was told by my faculty that I've lost the faculty perspective, and the academic vice president keeps telling me that I've got to stop thinking like a faculty member. What they don't realize is that I have to do both.''

The last comment highlights the difficulties deans face. Perhaps more than any other individuals in the organization, deans operate in the different cultural worlds that the faculty and administration have created for one another. Their job is one of constant interpretation of one constituency to another. The point is not that one dean is successful and another is unsuccessful, or that the job of a dean is critical or unimportant to the institution. Instead, the earlier discussion of administrators as individuals who are both subjects and objects, enmeshed in a cultural web that they help weave, may be elaborated on. The argument advanced here is that an administrator's impact is primarily with regard to cultural and symbolic actions. And these cultural and symbolic acts are inevitably tied to the ideology of the culture and the interpretation given it by the administrator.

Although it may be true that deans make similar instrumental decisions, it is apparent from the above comments that deans, chief academic officers, and presidents have widely varying impacts on the interpretive side of the organization. It is highly conceivable that, faced with a particular budgetary request, deans will arrive at a similar decision. Such a view supports much of the recent work of Cohen and March (1974), Weick (1976), and Birnbaum (1988). However, how a dean interprets and implements the decision and how someone interacts on a daily basis will vary as widely as we have seen in this chapter. To fashion such a view means that we must take into account how administrative decisions restructure the culture, and how the culture constrains administrative action. Instead of abstract management principles that a dean might follow, organizational meaning continually occurs on a day-to-day level so that even the most microscopic activities of an administrator's day take on meaning. William Foster is helpful in outlining how we might think of administrative action:

The context of administration requires that an administrative science be reconstructed as a moral science. An administrative science *can* be empirical, but also must incorporate hermeneutic (the science of interpreting and understanding others) and critical dimensions. Social science has increasingly recognized that it must be informed by moral questions: the paradigm of natural science does not apply when dealing with human issues. As a moral science, the science of administration is concerned with the resolution of moral dilemmas (1986, p. 24).

From this standpoint, administration has to do with the development of beliefs, values, attitudes, and commitment of the organizational participants. Administration is not so much precisely defined activities as a manner of directing human action. Surely the symbolic and instrumental activities of an organization are linked, but as discussed in Chapter 2, in the past we have tended to concentrate on measures that gauge *effectiveness*, rather than values, sentiments, or beliefs.

In Part IV we will return to a discussion of culture, power, authority, and ideology, and we will revisit the seven institutions a final time. My purpose will be to expand on the notion of administrative leadership mentioned here, to reconsider the curriculum as a cultural product, and to outline alternative avenues for faculty and administrators to explore within their organizations.

IV

Transformative Leadership

We have frequently printed the word democracy. Yet I cannot too often repeat that it is a word, the real gist of which still sleeps, quite unawaken'd, not withstanding the resonance and the many angry tempests out of which its syllables have come, from pen or tongue. It is a great word, whose history, I suppose, remains unwritten, because that history has yet to be enacted.

Walt Whitman
Democratic Vistas

7

Summing Up: Culture and the Curriculum

As I conclude the interview and both the respondent and I move toward his office door he pauses and says, "I'd like to make a comment about your interviewing style." My heart beats a little faster; I raise my eyebrows and await his comment. "I feel as if I've just spent an hour with my therapist. I've talked about things I normally don't talk about. It feels great! And it didn't even cost me $100!" We both laugh and take leave of one another.

The interviewee and the others with whom I have spoken speak with poignancy. Kuh and Whitt have commented that "the academy is rich in symbols, stories, and nuances of language that differentiate colleges and universities from one another and from other societal institutions. Yet these codes are essentially unexamined in the literature" (1988, p. 36). One aim of this research has been to uncover the "symbols, stories, and nuances." Indeed, a primary intent of cultural research is to bring the reader "in touch with the lives of strangers . . . and in some extended sense of the term to converse with them" (Geertz, 1973, p. 24).

It is important to understand the cultural life of an institution in order to assess what we want from postsecondary organizations and their curricula as we approach the twenty-first century. In large part, the curricular reports of the 1980s seldom asked basic questions: How do constituencies develop curricular initiatives? How do faculty and administrators define their relationship to one another, to their institutions, and to society? Instead, reformers lept to answering their own questions: What should the curriculum look like? What books should students read? How can postsecondary organizations be more effective? By asking their own questions and providing their own answers, the reformers have created a recipe for failure. When institutional participants balk at the curricular initiatives presented to them, or they reject thinking of the curriculum in terms of effectiveness measures, the reformers are able to place the blame for the failure to reform the curriculum at the feet of higher educators. Presidents lack leadership ability, academic vice presidents misunderstand how to manage change, and the faculty have a failure of nerve, are some of the criticisms that have been leveled at the higher education community.

My assumption is that to understand what to implement and how to implement change we must first comprehend the cultural determinants of postsecondary organizations. We have spoken of culture as a web in which the participants are entangled. We have attempted to excavate what Geertz has called "an ethnography of modern thought." He elaborates on what such an undertaking unearths:

> It will deepen even further our sense of the radical variousness of the way we think now, because it will extend our perception of that variousness beyond the merely professional realms of subject matter, method, technique, scholarly tradition and the like, to the larger framework of our moral existence. The conception . . . forging some general "the best that is being thought and said" ideology and working it into the curriculum, will then seem not merely implausible but utopian altogether (1983, p. 161).

Clearly, we have heard the "radical variousness" of different people's conceptions of the curriculum, knowledge and the cultures in which they live. It is now pertinent to ask: what, if any, common bonds do these individuals and institutions have? Is it possible to construct a unified framework of our moral existence when the organizational participants and institutions conceive of their existence in such fundamentally different ways? My assumption is that "the larger framework of our moral existence" in American higher education inevitably concerns the nurturing and promotion of democracy. As I noted at the outset of this work, democracy is a difficult topic to define, yet it is the fulcrum upon which college and university purpose resides. By speaking of democracy and democratic principles I have not meant to imply that a set of formal rules exist, such as that good citizens vote and bad citizens do not. As I have used it in this work, democracy concerns the manner in which organizational participants define and come to terms with the principles of social justice, equality, diversity, and empowerment. Empowerment concerns the ability of creating for students a curricular experience that enables them to see how society has created them, how the ideology of society has socialized them into the structures of the state, how their own unique histories fit and do not fit within society, and what they might do to lead an independent existence and to struggle for a better world.

I endorse the concept of democratic pluralism in higher education wherein different institutions will have different interpretations of democracy. As with traditional cultures, the cultures of organizations will have diverse interpretations of their histories and ideologies. Institutional mission statements need not rigidly define democracy. As we have seen, the meaning and curricular implications of an institutional commitment to democracy will be debated and acted on in a variety of ways. The essential point is that such debates take place. My assumption is that it is imperative that curricular proposals are framed as promoting some defensible sense of democracy, yet how those proposals are actually framed and enacted will differ from institution to institution.

In essence, the difficult task of the organizational participants of defining common goals and coming to terms with what bonds of social obligation exist for them is also the task of the researcher. To understand the larger framework of our moral existence, I first have to try to comprehend the nature of the web of organizational culture and the manifold voices that make up that culture. As author/observer I am entwined by the gossamer of the web. By structuring the argument in this vein I have taken a distinct departure from other works about the curriculum in higher education. We have seen portraits of how participants in seven institutions experience the cultural realities of their daily lives and how those realities influence the curriculum. By employing the methodology of critical ethnography, individuals in the same organization have spoken who promote ideas that are often inconsistent with one another, but nevertheless highlight the multiple voices at work in any organization. The attempt, then, has been to analyze how the culture of higher education organizations structures the way we think and talk about the curriculum. Taken into consideration has been the larger society in which the organizations exist, as well as the individuals who work within the organizations.

The Appendix discusses the measures employed to ensure accuracy when undertaking case studies of this nature. It is important to emphasize here the assumption of critical theorists about the relationship between methodology and theory. By accentuating the interrelatedness between theoretical suppositions and the way the researcher conducts research, critical theorists have been criticized for being subjective; the charge is that critical theorists choose data that best suit their theory. The assumption of critical theorists is that all data are inherently subjective. The questions a researcher asks and the answers a researcher uncovers are either implicitly or explicitly linked to theoretical formulations the researcher has about the world. The challenge for the critical theorist is to make those formulations explicit and show how the data either fit or do not fit the theory, so that further studies will be refined and reformulated. Thus, in this work a multitude of voices have helped to frame the discussion.

We now return to these voices. The remainder of this chapter will be divided into two parts. First we will reconsider culture and ideology in order to discuss how both terms interface with the mission and curriculum of the seven institutions. Second, we will discuss how power and authority operate within the constituencies of the faculty and administrators.

CULTURE AND IDEOLOGY

Each of the institutions has unique cultures wherein participants come to terms with the curriculum. The culture derives its meaning in large part through the ideological construction of the mission. As employed here, ideology concerns both the production and interpretation of meaning through the enactment of culture. The beliefs and values that organizational participants use to shape the curriculum derive in part from the mission. The importance of understanding the ideological significance of organizational mission concerns both the participants' ability to come to terms with how the organization produces meaning, and how the participants support, contradict, or resist those meanings. For example, the comprehension of how ideology works enables us to investigate the assumptions of the organizational participants' definition of knowledge and what should or should not go into a curriculum. We have seen several institutional interpretations of a mission. Christian University, for example, frames its mission by a religious ideology that participants consciously interpret as they build a curriculum and teach. Certain courses or subject matter are taboo. It is inconceivable that a biology course would discuss abortion counseling in a morally neutral tone. A literature course that offered the works of gay writers is similarly implausible.

We can also assume that most of the curriculum that Cutting Edge College offers would not be given at Christian University and vice versa. Interestingly, the ideologies of both Christian and Cutting Edge are similar in the direction they provide for organizational participants as they devise the curriculum. As with Christian, Cutting Edge College locates what goes on in the classroom with their mission. "A conservative, macho economist wouldn't make it here," comments a longtime faculty member. Presumably the faculty member objects not because the individual is an economist, or male, but because "conservative" and "macho" are words that run counter to the ethos of the institution. Similarly, a radical feminist will not be found teaching at Christian University. And the actions that occur as conservative or radical are often acted out on the terrain of the curriculum as the participants decide who best fits as professors, and what counts as academic knowledge. Hence, the interrelatedness of culture and ideology becomes evident.

The ideological nature of the mission should not be interpreted as a monolithic structure that all participants receive and similarly interpret. Clearly, the impact of the participants' previous experiences and the structures of academic disciplines also impact on how individuals interpret the mission. Individuals' histories influence the interpretations that take place. The disciplines interact with institutional ideologies so that academic knowledge both shapes and is shaped by the ideology of the institution. In this light, disciplines are not random formations; they reflect the historical, social, and organizational necessities that occur in culture. At the same time, disciplines are not determinist; they are not natural forms that simply evolved, but instead are the production of different social and cultural convergences.

From a critical perspective, ideologies contain both positive and negative possibilities. The central question is whether reflexive thought and action occur among the organizational participants. As a negative effect, ideology impresses upon people a singular interpretation of the way the world works so that they have little, if any, chance of self-questioning or thinking about the relationship of their learning to their own place in the world. On a positive side, ideology contains elements of reflexivity wherein organizational participants are encouraged to think about their own lives and their unique relationship to the world.

At Cutting Edge College, organizational participants constantly question the nature of what they are doing. It appears that all actions refer to the nature of the mission. The point, as one individual puts it, "is that we fundamentally question how knowledge has been structured. We are attempting to illuminate for students not knowledge as facts, but as inquiry, as a means to question and build their own lives." At Testimony State College the academic vice president adds, "Faculty get involved here even over where a parking lot should go. We constantly talk. Testimony makes slow decisions. We're not a bureaucracy, but a community that always turns inward and thinks how an act relates to who we are." And Testimony's discussions about matters such as parking lots and the like bring into focus for the participants the abstraction of institutional ideology. More than any other institution under study, participants at Christian University have concerned themselves with socializing students toward a particular worldview. Even so, younger faculty seek alternative ways to infuse Christianity into the curriculum. Advises one faculty member:

We should be working within a broadly Christian framework. What does it mean to be a Christian? The standard by which we should see if we're doing okay is to see how the curriculum illuminates our understanding of our own lives. We should have sharply competing points of view that force students to reflect.

Other faculty echo the speaker's comments. Even though they are in the minority, the example highlights how an institution's ideology contributes both positive and negative experiences. Some faculty members see their curriculum in relation to explicit ideological standards of self-reflection and praxis rather than socialization and indoctrination. The examples from all three institutions also demonstrate how the curriculum is a primary text upon which faculty act out the mission's beliefs. Even at Testimony State where the issue may concern a parking lot, the participants relate the discussion back to what they want from their school. As an abstraction, the mission demands interpretation. How the participants make sense of the abstraction provides a wealth of information about how they view knowledge, what a curriculum is, and the importance of democracy as it relates to the institution's culture.

Even at institutions where the institutional mission is apparently weak, individuals still need to make sense of the organization. By objectivizing the abstraction, the participants necessarily create a discourse about the relationship between mission and curriculum. For example, at Entrepreneurial College the ramifications of a mission that allows people to interpret what the institution is about in a multitude of ways highlights a radically different conception of knowledge than that found at either Cutting Edge or Christian. Attempts to change the curriculum at Entrepreneurial have been unsuccessful, faculty have serious disagreements with one another, and junior faculty are unsure about the tasks they are supposed to accomplish.

Each problem at Entrepreneurial logically follows from the mission's lack of an explicit path for the institution. Never sure of what they should be doing, faculty members have inaugurated several different models of what knowledge is and the curriculum could be. Faculty interpret the institution through the weakest of institutional ties, so that the other cultures of the faculty play a more prominent role than at institutions such as Christian or Testimony State. Since different disciplines have alternative visions of what educated students are, the faculty have violent disagreements. The loosest of common bonds tie the faculty together, so that they make sense of their organizational culture through their individual affiliations both within the institution and, beyond it, in the disciplines.

To be sure, a weak institutional association provides opportunities that are not evident elsewhere. The term coined for this institution is most appropriate—entrepreneurial. Entrepreneurial has a potpourri of curricular initiatives that have not had to have the consent of the entire faculty; instead, small cadres of faculty have gotten together and created different programs that interest them. A high degree of individual and departmental innovation has occurred. Curricula and forms of knowledge that a student would never be exposed to at either Testimony State or Classics, for example, will be found at Entrepreneurial. "A student who comes here has a lot of choices," comments one individual. Another says, "It's great for the faculty. If you really want something you can do it. There aren't many constraints."

Although it is true that pockets exist for faculty and students to experiment in, Entrepreneurial's participants appear to want a more uniform interpretation of social definition. Recall the students who commented on their desire for "synthesis." The scientist surely wanted a more "rigorous" curriculum that was less politically motivated. Another individual spoke sadly about the failures of previous all-college curricular initiatives. One individual adds, "If you're asking me if I'm content with what we offer, the answer is no. If you're asking me if I think we can agree on what we should do, the answer is also no."

The institution affords organizational participants both positive and negative ideological moments. Entrepreneurial allows individuals the freedom to think about how their own work and their own teaching relates to defining knowledge and how they might be concerned with democracy. In some respects, the highly individualist philosophy of the institution may force more critical reflection than elsewhere because Entrepreneurial's participants do not have any institutional guideposts telling them what they are doing is right or wrong. At the same time, inasmuch as critical reflection on what they should be doing does not have to exist, discussions of the relationship of knowledge to democracy, or how to define knowledge, do not have to take place. Proponents of the model may well advocate Emerson's dictum that "consistency is the hobgoblin of little minds." The question, however, is not if an institutional mission must enforce rigid curricular structures and definitions of knowledge but, rather, whether a mission aids all individuals in becoming reflective citizens. The question thus becomes how Entrepreneurial might provide its participants with opportunities to think about their own relationship to knowledge and still maintain their organizational identity.

Working Class State College is in a similar dilemma. In one respect a public institution has an explicit mission to serve the needs of the working-class people of the state. Yet a mission that was clear and singularly interpreted when public institutions began no longer means very much to faculties who come primarily from research universities and have a diversity of interests. Within given parameters, the participants at Working Class almost act as if they can create the ideology for the institution *tabula rasa*. The accreditation team, for example, is not using previous mission statements as they go about defining the future of Working Class. The new academic vice president borrows from his experiences at a radically different institution to try to remake

Working Class. One individual went so far as to compare a religious institution where he had been with Working Class State. If an organizational participant cannot find a difference between the missions of secular and religious institutions, then upon what basis do the organizational participants in the public college build their curriculum?

As with many institutions, the course offerings of Working Class have grown as faculty have added courses that they want to teach. When faculty stop offering the course, it most often is not deleted. Unlike Entrepreneurial College, there is not much evidence that faculty have attempted to develop curricular offerings as a composite whole. At Entrepreneurial, for example, some faculty have put together a unified freshman-year experience. Other faculty have created a particular theme that students can study. At Working Class students learn in a piecemeal fashion from course to course. As one student points out, "We get our learning sort of like building blocks. We never see the whole thing." The underlying assumption, of course, is that a "whole thing" exists. Such an assumption is in keeping with Classics' mission, and is also held by some faculty at Entrepreneurial. The faculties at Cutting Edge and Testimony deny the assumption that knowledge can ever be studied as a "whole thing." In this respect, Working Class State exemplifies many institutions that operate on the belief that knowledge is a concrete entity that is translated into an institutional curricula. Students are introduced to separate facets of knowledge but, more often than not, they do not see how the pieces fit together, or how all of the pieces relate to their lives.

Instead, at Working Class State, students and faculty alike equate education with jobs. Much like Paulo Freire's banking theory of education (1970), organizational participants look on higher education from the perspective that students are consumers of knowledge, of static facts that have little relationship to their lives, in order that they gain a certificate at the end of the process that will show employers they are qualified to work. As noted previously, the explicit class-based relationship of a public institution creates a culture that reproduces the inequalities found in society. Students from the working class need jobs and, unlike the graduates of Classics or Entrepreneurial, few assurances or fallbacks are there if collegiate training fails to qualify them for work. The process often seems void of positive moments of ideological turmoil and struggle. Presumably, John Dewey had Working Class's form of education in mind when he asked: "What avail is it to win prescribed

amounts of geography and history, to win the ability to read and write
. . . if he loses desire to apply what he has learned and, above all, loses
the ability to extract meaning from his future experiences as they occur?'' (1963, p. 49).

Up to this moment curricular change at Working Class State has come
from an external authority—the state. To an extent, the designation of
international studies as a specialty area has enhanced the atmosphere
for the faculty and students. ''The [state] secretary of education,'' relates
one individual, ''said at a meeting in the capital last week that more
students per institution go abroad here than at any other institution in
the country.'' Even though the assertion is implausible, and several
individuals note that it probably is not true, many people also mention
that the secretary of education has singled them out. Students also claim
that they are pleased to have the opportunity to go abroad but, in the
next breath, they say they have no plans to utilize the option.

Thus, even with a curricular offering of which they can express pride,
the organizational participants have built little positive ideological momentum. Students and faculty speak of what the individual learned
abroad; but knowledge concerns facts and figures or the barest of tour-
istlike intangibles, such as the tautological recognition that different
countries are different. What is lacking is the ability of such a program
to aid students in their understanding of America's place in the world,
and the appreciation of the diversity of cultures. Presumably, sensitivity
to other cultures will help students become more open-minded to differences within their own culture. A program such as the one at Working
Class State has positive ideological possibilities. The unique aspect of
the program is that it allows students to go abroad who otherwise might
never see another country. For example, when I spoke with students at
Entrepreneurial and Cutting Edge, many of them casually mentioned
they already had traveled abroad either with their families or friends.
The financial opportunity of Working Class State's program affords
students a chance for experiences they would otherwise not have. But
the institution capitalizes on the program clumsily.

Finally, a relationship with the community is virtually nonexistent at
Working Class State. Although the institution offers continuing education classes and the like, a concerned involvement in the economic
development of a town in a recession, with unemployment, is not apparent. In some respects, one might say that the mission of the institution
fits a quite traditional mold of educational purpose—to socialize youth

into the mainstream of society, and to provide students with the requisite skills for employment. Yet what can a public institution like Working Class State do? Surely the parents and students at the institution want learning to be equated with jobs.

Giroux and McLaren elaborate on the kind of education students experience at Working Class, and an alternative trail Working Class State's participants might attempt to chart:

> The ideological shift at work here points to a restricted definition of schooling, one that almost completely strips public education of a democratic vision where citizenship and the politics of possibility are given serious consideration. . . . We mean that primacy is given to education as an economic investment, that is, to pedagogical practices designated to create a school-business partnership and make the American economic system more competitive in world markets. A politics of possibility and citizenship, by contrast, refers to a conception of schooling in which classrooms are seen as active sites of public intervention and social struggle (1986, p. 221).

It is certainly possible to paint heroic and villainous pictures of collegiate institutions. However, the painting of such portraits is futile. I am more concerned with exhibiting how culture and ideology interact in postsecondary institutions and with outlining how the curriculum is a cultural text. Institutions grapple with pieces of a problem one at a time; the dilemma for organizational participants is deciding which piece of which problem to struggle with. The challenge for Working Class State is that they must struggle with several different pieces at the same time. As a new administrative team tries to create different curricular offerings, they also must redefine who their clientele is, where the local community fits into the equation, and what kinds of relationships should take place between faculty and administration. And these issues are above and beyond the normal everyday dilemmas that higher educators face, such as maintaining the facilities, upgrading the library, and balancing the budget. The problems at Working Class State are endemic to most public state colleges and universities. I submit that rather than attack problems on the micro level of curricular offerings, such institutions might benefit in uncovering the general nature of their relationship to the state and, of consequence, the ideological apparatus of their cultures. In turn, they can then go about implementing their own unique conceptions of knowledge into a curriculum based on institutional mission.

This is working from the assumption that the mission plays a more determined role than previously thought. At one time researchers believed only those institutions with sagas as defined by Clark (1980) provided intensive guidelines from which participants found meaning and identity. I suggest that institutional ideology goes much farther; even in institutions where a clearly delineated saga is not apparent, the strength of what the mission says or does not say helps define the parameters for action and discourse. Most often, action and discourse occur on the terrain of curricular planning. The language that people use and the discussions that are held surrounding curricular change locate specific social practices and relations. Such discussions ultimately link up to the relationships between ideology and culture. The curriculum, then, is neither only a tool to be used to increase the economic welfare of the nation, nor is it only a set of developmental building blocks from which a socialized American emerges. The curriculum is the locale for debating what it means to be American in the late twentieth century, and of consequence, what it means to live in a democracy.

POWER AND AUTHORITY

As we have seen, throughout an organization's culture, the organizational participants experience power and authority. We will first consider authority within the cultures of Christian University and Testimony State College, and then discuss power at the colleges of Classics and Women's. How the institutions etch their figures of authority and conceive of power affords insight into the institutional concern for democracy and citizenship.

The central dilemma upon which these examples turn is the institutional participants' ability and will to challenge themselves. How do people learn to question authority? What are the parameters of discourse within which reflective inquiry may occur? One of the paradoxes of authority in a democracy is that education must teach students when to challenge authority. Diversity in a democracy is a necessary ingredient, although times occur when particular forms of diversity are unacceptable, for they threaten the fabric of society. For example, as a society we reject a concept of authority where one group enslaves another group, as in South Africa. Yet clear-cut examples do not always exist. How does one learn when or when not to challenge authority? Nyberg and Farber expand on this point:

The means for achieving common understanding is conversation within and between communities. We mean the kind of conversation open to all persons and all subjects that can profitably be discussed, but not entirely or radically free conversation. Profitable talk is never entirely free of constraints. There must be rules of the game, and teachers must teach what they are (1986, pp. 11–12).

We have seen different appeals to authority in the unique cultures of the seven institutions. Christian University's form of institutional authority says little about issues such as social justice or empowerment. Instead, authority concerns the doctrines of the church and the Bible as interpreted and lived in the twentieth century. For example, because an individual is a teacher, the individual will have attributed authority because he or she has knowledge. In this light, authority is the idea that different individuals hold authority either because of the nature of their position or because they are knowledgeable about a particular topic. We can say, then, that an individual is in a "position of authority," or that an individual is an "authority on the subject."

This view of authority, cloaked in the culture of the organization, calls for portraits of faculty as purveyors of knowledge to students, and administrators as technicians who know how to make the organization run smoothly. What we do not gain from this picture is a sense of how a student or another organizational participant learns to question or challenge authority. A singular worldview exists of what is "good" and faculty and administrators are the individuals charged with the transmission of the worldview. In essence, what we have done is reify an idea—authority—so that we come to believe that, for one reason or another, a particular individual equals authority.

Consider the ramifications of such a conception of authority. Individuals are authorities because they hold knowledge. Knowledge, then, is a mass, a static entity that some have and others do not. Seen in this perspective, students cannot be participants in a learning experience; instead, students learn from those who have knowledge. Students cannot challenge what they learn because the assumption is that they do not have the conceptual tools to engage in such a challenge. Thus, knowledge is also seen as something that is apolitical. For example, the assumption at Christian University is that individuals gain authority because they have followed the basic tenets of their religion which calls for spiritual fulfillment that is divorced from earthly concerns. Referential learning where students strive to engage in a process whereby they locate themselves within larger social realities does not occur; learning takes place where students reproduce those realities.

Testimony State College calls the concept of authority into question. In this view authority is inextricably linked to the idea of dissolving figures of authority and instead providing organizational participants with a set of educational practices that enable students to be active participants in their future. From this perspective faculty remain as knowledgeable individuals, but instead of all-knowing, they emerge as co-learners with students. An example from Testimony State provides insight. A variety of student voices combine to speak quite distinctly of their education and their learning experience. One student begins by speaking about the faculty: "They want to learn too. I feel like a colleague with the faculty, rather than just a student. That whole stigma of not being able to talk with your professors doesn't exist here. We're supposed to talk; it's part of this place."

"I appreciate that you can negotiate your education," adds an additional student. "You can create your education so that ultimately it benefits, it makes sense to you." Another student concurs, "It's almost in the purest form like a traditional education. They're getting you to learn what it means to learn. Not just facts and figures." An adult student notes, "It's up to me to make the program challenging. It's up to the students to learn. I've got to make it challenging for myself." When asked if this kind of education is for everyone, virtually all of the students agree: "Everyone couldn't make it here. High achievers who want to compete wouldn't like this place. And if you want to just sit back and not think, the faculty will challenge you, they'll fight you on it."

As with Christian University, students mention the consistent use of values by their teachers. "I haven't had a class yet where an instructor hasn't brought ethics into the discussion. The lack of ethics in business, I don't see how values don't get wrapped up in everything we do, we study." One student says, "We're really taught to think on our own, come to our own decisions." An African American student disagrees, "I'd just like to say that from a person of color's perspective there is only one perspective taught here—white people's. And if we get different viewpoints, it's usually from a faculty of color." A woman student asks, "Are male faculty really concerned about women's issues? I wonder. Sometimes I think male and female faculty are in the same class so that some of the men faculty don't have to be concerned with women's issues. That's wrong.''

Although values are taught, a distinct difference exists between the two paths that Christian and Testimony State have chosen to walk down. Even though some of the students voice dissatisfaction with the lack of a person of color's perspective or a lack of male professors' attention to women's issues, notice that the students voice their concerns and they are willing to challenge the institution. The trail at Testimony State necessitates that students "think on our own, come to our own decisions." The professors are authorities in the sense that they have particular expertise in certain areas; rather than purveyors of knowledge, they are guides along a trail upon which they have not travelled. Students defer to the faculty as we would any guides, yet essentially the role of the professoriate is to empower students rather than socialize them to the singular teachings of a particular system.

I should not overdraw the distinction between Testimony and Christian. Some faculty at Christian undoubtedly try to make their students question their relationship to what they are learning, and some faculty will try to make students co-learners. It would also be facile to suggest that because Testimony's faculty goes about their work in a radically different manner than at most other institutions that the faculty has done away with an authority relationship. In essence, I agree with a senior faculty member at Testimony State:

Given the nature of the relationship—faculty to student—I would be deceiving myself if I didn't think that power and authority still exist here. You have to think about where we are, at what time and place in our history. What's important is that I recognize the relationship is built on that, and that I expose students to the nature of the relationship and we work at it. We constantly work at it here. That's what's so exciting—and so exhausting!

Participants in an organization who view authority as if it encapsulates knowledge will necessarily view power in a similar light. Power will be seen as residing with an individual or office so that we can say a person is a "powerful individual" or that a particular role in an organization is a "powerful position." It follows that proponents of this position will not believe that a struggle over the curriculum is essentially a political struggle—that the curriculum is a political process that involves a fight over the power relations that structure the wider society.

A return to Classics College will aid in our understanding. "The place has been governed by a powerful educational ideology," states one longtime faculty member. "There's an ethic, a set of values, that articulate what we believe is important to know." The assumption at Classics College is that a curriculum reflects what a faculty believes to be the accumulated wisdom of society. The curriculum is not vocational in the sense of learning a skill; the curriculum teaches people how to think. A student is an educated person when one has mastered the curricular content.

When faculty speak of the curriculum at Classics College, they do not discuss power, except as in reference to positional influence. Particular people hold power, they can stymie change. But the perception is that faculty deliberations about knowledge and the curriculum are not a discourse about power relations; instead, the discussions concern what one needs to know to function intellectually and to think critically in society. Although the college community rejects any aspect of vocational training such as is found at Working Class State, the classical curriculum reflects a similar relationship to power as takes place at Working Class. A concern for understanding power and how it works is nonexistent. As with vocational education, the paramount concern is to create individuals who can function—in this case, intellectually—in society according to a prescribed formula.

One camp at Women's College also assumes that the curriculum should reflect what the faculty believe to be the necessary intellectual qualities of a college student. Neither these faculty nor the faculty at Classics believe that knowledge is static. "The knowledge in my discipline has exploded. I have trouble keeping up," admitted the biochemist. As breakthroughs in knowledge are made, the curriculum must change. Yet change occurs not because of the power relations exerted on the curriculum, but through a rational problem-solving process.

The faculty in the other camp at Women's College conceptualize power in a different light. They believe that the curriculum cannot be divorced from a study of power insofar as the curriculum suggests how different constituencies construct their social reality. Their view is similar to that of Foucault, who comments:

Education may well be . . . the instrument whereby every individual . . . can gain access to any kind of discourse. But we well know that in its distribution, in what it permits and what it prevents, it follows the well-trodden battle lines of social conflict. Every education system is a political means of maintaining or of modifying the appropriation of discourse (1972, p. 277).

The implications of Foucault's comment are that teaching and learning are directly linked to power. The curriculum represents a struggle for meaning and control over one's life. Rather than neutral, the curriculum is a value-laden construct that helps determine relations of power.

Power. Authority. Ideology. Culture. By now it should be apparent that I find it fruitless to isolate these concepts as if they were mutually exclusive. Although each term is abstract, difficult to comprehend, and worthy of more space than I have provided, the central object of study has been the construction of the collegiate curriculum.

As opposed to some theorists who use culture as a simile—an organization is *like* a culture—I have used it as a synonym—an organization *is* a culture. A culture has an ideology that helps determine both how power exists in the organization and how conceptions of authority get played out. An institution's mission is the clearest example of an ideology. Different conceptions of power and authority are reflected in how curricular change occurs, who controls the change, and what changes take place.

A central tenet has been that organizational participants construct their realities and are constructed by the mediating influences of the larger society, the organization itself, and the multitude of individuals and relationships that take place within the organization. Culture, ideology, power, and authority both determine and are determined by individual action. In turn, individuals are both subjects and objects who are created by and create their culture. As a cultural artifact, the curriculum is also socially constructed. Given the assumption that individuals can transform their reality, what strategies might organizational participants use to enhance democracy and citizenship? In the final chapter we will consider this question.

8

Transformative Leadership and the Democratic Imperative

In earlier chapters three junior faculty expressed confusion about their roles, about whether they should be primarily teachers or researchers. An academic vice president voiced concern at the number of meetings he had to attend, and a president was unsure of how to relate to his faculty. A professor "scooted" around the administration to effect curricular change, and a second academic vice president wished the faculty could better understand the differences between policy and management. A student was disappointed that he had never had the opportunity to synthesize the "whole thing" and another student commented on the loneliness he felt as he struggled to understand his relationship to "the whole thing."

The disparate voices and their shifting concerns produce a cacophony of values. To complicate matters, if we returned to the institutions today we would undoubtedly find different dilemmas and different voices. The denial of tenure to three people may well have receded into the corners of Entrepreneurial's culture; perhaps a new president at Classics College has brought many underlying curricular issues to the forefront. Tension may have lessened at Women's College, while strain may have heightened at Christian University. Surely, new issues also have arisen that were of little concern when I visited.

A cultural study of seven institutions can neither predict the next adventures at the colleges, nor generalize about how administrators and faculty should operationalize their missions and curricula. It has been my intent to highlight the voices and words of the organizational participants in these seven institutions in order to think about how they construct the curriculum, and what strategies they might utilize to work toward democracy. Problems, as they exist in a culture, are never the same. They change from moment to moment, and are different within each context. It is futile to try to invent causally determined solutions to the dilemmas that humans confront in organizations. We can, however, approach institutional life with particular visions of what we want from the organization, both for ourselves and as an overall organizational goal.

At the start of this work I spoke of a climb to Wilson Peak, 14,110 feet into the Colorado sky, and a hike into Chaco Canyon, home of the Anasazi. We are never sure what we will encounter en route to a high mountain summit or into a desert canyon. A summer storm and lightning can flash unexpectedly, stranding us on a mountain cliff or turning a dry creek bed into a raging torrent. The multitude of flowers on a summer hillside can blind us with dazzling beauty. We may spot an eagle soaring magnificently in the canyon, or we might fall into an icy mountain creek as we stumble off a log. The process of mountain climbing and hiking is always different, always rich with difficulty and promise.

It might be beneficial to approach academic work in a similar manner. To be sure, we all want to avoid a lightning storm and we can take precautions, but ultimately we are no more in command of our own cultures than we are of nature's elements. Academic work holds boundless possibilities. The processes in which we are involved are always different and rich with difficulty and promise. What might we do to reach a summit? How might we enliven our experiences so that we also achieve a democratic vista similar to what Katharine Lee Bates beheld atop Pikes Peak?

This chapter will consider three points. First it offers suggestions about how we might conceptualize academic problems in culture. Second, a concept of cultural leadership for faculty and administrators is discussed. Third, a few ideas are advanced about how to address academic problems.

APPROACHING ACADEMIC LIFE

To assume that postsecondary organizations have goals similar to other social institutions provides a different picture of colleges and universities than to think about the distinctions between the university and other organizations. I work from the assumption that postsecondary organizations are unique entities that have goals and concerns that extend far beyond measures of effectiveness and efficiency. Laws of supply and demand will play into an institution's decision to create a particular curriculum, as will other criteria; but the overarching purpose of institutional life concerns bonds of social obligation that relate to what I have called "the democratic imperative."

An educational organization's purpose in a democracy is more than to survive in a difficult environment or to produce the human capital necessary to meet the manpower needs of the state. Higher education's purpose is in some form or shape to foment democracy, to foster and expand the democratic experience. The idea advanced here is that one overriding message of colleges and universities should be a rededication to the diversity of people who make up the United States. I am proposing that the essence of postsecondary education is a concern that is grounded in forms of moral and ethical actions that consciously reach out to the diverse populations of America. Of consequence, postsecondary organizations will concern themselves not only with those who voice opinions, but also to the silent, to the dispossessed.

Building on Robert Wolff's (1969) work, Michael Katz offers a compelling analysis of what he terms "the ideal university, a community of learning." He declares that postsecondary organizations "Should be a community of persons united by collective understandings, by common and communal goals, by bonds of reciprocal obligation, and by a flow of sentiment which makes the preservation of the community an object of desire, not merely a matter of prudence or a command of duty" (1987, p. 179).

A definition of the goals of higher education such as the one Katz (and Wolff) provide necessitates an overt ideological commitment on the part of an organization's participants. What I hope I have shown in this work is that whether participants actively commit themselves to a specific ideology, within all cultures ideology is at work. The participants may be conscious of their ideological commitment such as at Christian University and Cutting Edge, or they may be unaware of their ideological stance, as at Entrepreneurial and Classics. Nevertheless, to speak of organizational culture, and human action within it, is to speak of the ideologies to which the participants commit themselves. Necessarily, then, organizational participants need to unearth the inherent assumptions at work in their missions and create an ongoing reflexive discourse that works toward achieving "collective understandings."

To advocate an overriding concern for democracy does not imply that all colleges and universities will march in lockstep with one another, offering similar curricula and programs. To the contrary, I assume that each of the institutions mentioned in this text will enact a vision of democracy that is different from one another; at the same time the institution's primary consideration will be to advance democracy. For example, Christian University, Working Class State, and Women's College will all have different constituencies, different decision-making structures, and different perceptions of the curriculum. However, my assumption is that when their institutional discourse is about democracy rather than capturing markets, or assuming a neutral view of knowledge, then the participants will move closer toward achieving collective understandings of what it means for their institution to participate in education for democracy. The collective understandings, because they are rooted in the cultures of the organizations and based on the participants' interpretations, will differ from institution to institution. Notwithstanding, the collective understandings will be embedded in a concern for democracy.

As the institutional analyses have shown, on a daily basis a multitude of perceptions and interpretations are constantly at work, and one person or group is not necessarily right and the other wrong. The message a president intends to convey to people may or may not be interpreted in the manner he or she has desired. People may not even interpret the message at all. If individuals have a multitude of perceptions and interpretations, then of particular concern for orchestrating organization action will be the collective understanding of an overarching organizational message.

Thus, the manner in which organizational participants might conceptualize and approach academic problems in culture is twofold. First, by accepting that all organizations operate within a cultural framework where an ideology exists, the participants need to uncover the basic tenets of their ideologies and think about how these ideologies define the nature of their academic life. Second, organizational participants need to take into account how the unique nature of their cultures foments democracy. I am suggesting that a principal concern of organizational participants is to come to terms with an understanding of democracy and how their organization's culture by way of the curriculum enhances democracy.

Suggestions of this kind frame the parameters of how organizational leaders might think about academic problems; a cultural view of colleges and universities premised on democracy presents particular challenges for leaders. Once leaders understand the nature of ideology, power, and authority in their organizations, what are they to do? Answering this question first requires an understanding of the meaning of leadership in such an organization.

TRANSFORMATIVE LEADERSHIP

James MacGregor Burns coined the term transformational leadership by stating that individuals who "shape, alter, or elevate the values and goals of followers through the vital teaching role" (1978, p. 425) are transformational leaders. Individuals such as Ghandi or Martin Luther King, Jr., come to mind as persons who led social movements and helped shape people's consciousness and realities.

In higher education, Cameron and Ulrich also have spoken of transformational leadership, but they have used the term as a synonym for any kind of effective change agent. They have looked at leaders who are capable of transforming the institution irrespective of ideology. They state, "Transformational leaders create a readiness for change among their followers, manage the natural resistance to new conditions and new requirements, and articulate a vision of the future that mobilizes commitment and creates successful institutionalization throughout the system" (1986, p. 12). From this perspective a transformational leader is someone who can transform an institution; a concern for someone who can "shape, alter, or elevate the values" of followers is absent in their definition.

I am concerned with transformational leadership as defined by Burns and utilized by all organizational participants. In this light, transformative leadership concerns the ability of individuals or groups to structure organizational discourse around the nature of social relations and values, and a concern for creating a community of critical, reflective citizens. If organizational life and the curriculum represent a struggle for meaning, then I am calling for transformative leaders who are centrally concerned with issues of social justice and empowerment, whose overriding commitment is on behalf of the disadvantaged and silent. My point of departure with Burns is that transformative leaders do not necessarily have to be those few individuals in positions from which we have come to expect "leadership." I am not concerned with developing a notion of transformational leadership only for college and university presidents. Presidents need to exhibit transformative leadership, but within the web of culture, leadership is too organic and interrelated to be limited to only a particular role. The challenge is for all organizational participants to be transformative leaders who seek to "shape, alter, and elevate" the values of their colleagues.

Bennis comments:

The transformative power of leadership stems less from ingeniously crafted organizational structures, carefully constructed management designs and controls, elegantly rationalized planning formats, or skillfully articulated leadership tactics. Rather, it is the ability of the leader to reach the souls of others in a fashion which raises human consciousness, builds meanings, and inspires human intent. . . . Within transformative leadership, therefore, it is vision, purposes, beliefs, and other aspects of organizational culture that are of prime importance (1984, p. 70).

From this perspective, leadership is not a science, skill, or trait, but rather a way of directing an organizational culture toward a higher moral plane. Leadership may occur in any manner of styles or forms, given the nature of the organization's culture. Symbolic maintenance and the ability to interpret the culture both for the participants and of the participants becomes essential so that the leader comprehends how to "build meanings." Organizational purpose does not get defined in terms of static data, but around a dedication to a particular belief that is under constant reinterpretation. Language and symbols play a critical role in developing and maintaining organizational meaning so that transformative leadership is more strategic and less instrumental.

By defining leadership in this manner we posit that leaders cannot assume the posture of neutrality toward their institutions, cultures, and ideologies. Leadership involves more than effective managerial practices insofar as colleges and universities represent forms of knowledge, social relations, and values that are representative of society. Transformative leaders, then, are critically engaged in the ongoing definition of their organization and in the work of empowering all of the participants to help define the nature of their realities.

In each of these case studies, we have glimpsed transformative leaders and the struggles they encounter. In the autumn at Testimony State College the AVP points out, "I feel we have been making inadequate progress in hiring people of color. I've taken that on as a key task. We intend to hire more people of color and it will call on me not letting go." Remember the comment in the spring by a faculty member who said, "The AVP has begun to exert his own form of moral leadership." Another individual comments, "A year ago if I had said to him to exert moral leadership he would have laughed at me! That's a lot of learning on his part. Look at how he keeps the issue of the hiring of minorities as a central focus."

After a year's debate and much disagreement, the curriculum committee at Women's College puts out a document to the community that calls for dramatically different ways to think about the curriculum. In part the document states as emphases:

The goals of comparison and integration assert the educational importance of learning to view one's own and other cultures in a comparative way. This goal asks the student to stand outside of her primary cultures: racial, religious, ethnic, national, linguistic, temporal, and to learn to view them in a broader context. ... This goal also asks that a student be able to stand outside the 'culture' of her discipline, and to evaluate its questions, methods, modes of thoughts, values, and answers.

The report goes on to suggest that

teaching is an integral part of curriculum. The involvement of the student with the content to be learned, the development of her skills and perspectives, the ways in which she learns to question, compare, and value what she is learning are all integrally related to the aims and approaches of the teacher.

At Cutting Edge College a faculty member speaks about the institution:

You have to build mechanisms that reward particular kinds of things. We reward the values we hold to be our mission. Interdisciplinary work, dedication to teaching. It's a different sense of what teaching is about. Elsewhere students will say they took a course, or learned such and such. We want more. We want them to get in there and think about their own lives, about ideas, and see how they can change what's out there.

Each of these examples speaks of different forms of transformative leadership. An AVP—an individual—seeks to help the institution re-dedicate itself to a common concern for equity and affirmative action. A committee puts forth a document that calls into question the way they have previously organized curricular and pedagogical practice. An institution tries to engage its students in a form of inquiry that necessitates critical reflection.

Obviously, transformative leadership is not a panacea to all problems that take place in an institution. With each example, particular frustrations and disagreements arise. We recall how the AVP at Testimony State expresses frustration with the distinction between "policy and management." Two of the members of the curriculum committee at Women's College submit a statement of dissent about the document. Cutting Edge College is concerned about its retention rate and is unsure what to do, where to turn.

By taking responsibility for the purposes and conditions of education, transformative faculty and administrators strive to create a climate wherein the conditions of the community's existence are made clear. The curriculum is no longer a morally neutral object of socialization, but instead it is a construct that relates to how the organizational participants see the world. Rather than a curricular structure that is imposed solely from the past, transformative leaders seek to define the structure itself in light of present social contexts.

Much of the previous literature on leadership has concerned how to make rational choices based on quantifiable, analyzable data. Certainly there are times when leaders must utilize such data; and the utilization and manipulation of the data will help their institutions out of difficult problems. One of the most striking cultural signs that concerns academic strategy is the information or lack thereof that organizational participants call upon to inform their dilemmas. Organizations with quite strong academic cultures, such as Testimony State or Cutting Edge College, often seem to have a dim understanding of national trends or data. One benefit of the emphasis on effectiveness and efficiency in higher education over the last decade has been that much information about national trends has been accumulated that can help leaders make decisions.

Similarly, when a mountain climber plans to take a trip he or she is sure to take rain gear and an extra pair of socks. The hiker talks with a ranger about conditions of the trail and finds out from other hikers if there is better equipment to be used. Institutions that have intensive cultures often neglect individuals with whom they might speak or tools they might use. "I can't imagine an outsider being AVP here. We're so unique," mentions a person at Cutting Edge. Remember the professor at Testimony State who commented that people looked upon him as a neophyte who knew nothing when he entered the culture.

Ultimately, however, the information a leader draws upon is useless if the organization is unclear about its intentions and goals. Simply stated, warm socks may keep a hiker's feet dry on a mountain trail, but presumably the intent of a mountain climb is not to wander mindlessly up a path. What the seven case studies have shown is that the organizational participants often are unsure of what trail they are on and where they are going. A guidebook for transformative leaders is not yet in print, but the case studies imply some suggestions for transformative leadership.

ADDRESSING ACADEMIC ISSUES

Mission

We have emphasized the centrality of an organization's mission. As the overarching ideological apparatus of an organization's culture, a mission statement helps people make sense of who they are as an institution and where they want to go. Ideology offers a starting point for a discussion of the social and political interests of the institution. Further, a mission statement not only raises questions but also provides answers.

We need to expand our notions of what a mission is so that the organization's participants do not equate a mission simply with formulaic goals and objectives. A mission statement should incorporate the aspirations and hopes of the community. Mission statements link up an organization's history with present-day contexts to provide a vision of the future. The mission and ideology of a culture also help provide guidelines for action within the culture, while at the same time calling into question how specific activities might change in the future. For example, Christian University's mission affords participants an understanding of how the institution is different and unique from other institutions so that people have a sense of the parameters of culture. At the same time, due to the incorporation of new members and the changing societal and historical contexts, the mission serves as a referent for change so that the participants continually question how their work can relate to an ideology of what it means to be a faculty member or administrator in a Christian institution in the waning days of the twentieth century.

As I noted earlier, the point of discussing democracy and institutional mission does not imply a homogenization of all organizations. The seven institutions discussed here have unique missions that are often at variance with one another. Yet one value that ties all of these institutions together is that they are American institutions with their history and destiny inextricably tied to this country. Each institution should think about where it wants to go not only because of markets or niches that wait to be filled, or economic manpower needs that must be met, but also because of an institution's historical claim in American society.

The clearest and most difficult example of mission definition concerns public institutions. The history of public institutions has been tied to meeting the needs of the citizenry. Given that the state plays a fundamental role in defining institutional purpose, colleges such as Working Class State have come under a sustained pressure to meet the economic needs of business and industry. Although Testimony State is also a public institution, given their charter as an alternative institution, they have escaped the mandate of equating education with jobs. The clienteles of Working Class and Testimony are also different; the parents and students at Working Class expect their education to offer training that will lead to jobs, whereas Testimony's constituencies are not as concerned with job training. As public institutions such as Working Class plot out where they want to be in the twenty-first century, thoughtful discussions ought to be held around how the democratic imperative is incorporated into the text of the mission. The assumption is that colleges and universities can do more than provide jobs for their citizens.

It is also apparent that many religious institutions are at a crossroads. The distinctive flavor of what they are is threatened as they open themselves to different constituencies who care little for the religious doctrines of the institution. What it means to be Catholic or Baptist or Lutheran is also under serious debate from within the churches. Religious colleges and universities have a vital role to play in such a discussion. In essence, the dialogue should center around what the institution wants to become and how these institutions can foment conversations within their communities that foster the liberation of the spirit and soul. The institutions need to engage critically in a dialogue that concerns the nature of their own self-formation and participation in a democratic society.

The kind of discussion that Women's College has had concerning its mission is an example of the kind of dialogue from which institutions such as Entrepreneurial College and Classics College might also benefit. As observed at Women's College, such discussions are never easy. Different groups actively disagree with one another and arguments erupt at committee meetings and elsewhere. Faculty and administrators view one another with suspicion. At times the task of discussing "what we are about" seems overwhelming and a gratuitous waste of time. Nevertheless, such discussions are necessary. For example, the report of the curriculum committee at Women's College shows that they are on their way not only to articulating a mission statement, but also to demonstrating how the mission is linked to curricular objectives.

All levels of the institutions should engage in ongoing conversations about institutional mission. Mission statements should not be devised simply to placate an accrediting body's demand. Testimony State College and Cutting Edge College are examples of institutions where ongoing dialogues take place. At Testimony State the AVP comments, "Faculty even expect to be consulted about where a parking lot should go because they believe it will affect what we do." At Cutting Edge College we observed how the faculty constantly question if what they are doing relates to what the institution is about.

One of the paradoxes discovered during these case studies is that if one wants to develop a mission that means something tangible to institutional members such as at Testimony State and Cutting Edge, it will involve a considerable institutional and individual commitment. To take the time to talk about the mission implies that the institution will not talk about something else. The paradox is that not to talk about the mission denies participants a sense of organizational meaning. In this light, what I am calling for is an extension of Clark's notion of a saga to all institutions. He talks about the rewards:

An embodied idea is the institutional chariot to which individual motive becomes chained. When the idea is in command, men are indifferent to personal cost.

They often are not aware of how much they have risked and how much they have sacrificed. They are proud of what they have been through, what they have done, and what they stand for.... In such efforts, the task—and the reward—of the institutional leader is to create and initiate an activating mission (1980, p. 262).

Defining the ideology of the institution will foster a consistency that helps focus collective understandings in many areas of the college. Testimony State's job descriptions and hiring policies is an example of one organizational component that takes place with reference to what the institutional participants believe themselves to be. Christian University's policy that all members attend chapel and Cutting Edge's ethos of dropping in on one another for intellectual discussion and feedback are additional examples of how ideology focuses institutional activity. The socialization of new members to the organization takes on increased importance. How faculty, students, and administrators learn about the mores and values of the organization frame for them how they are to act in the organization. All too often socialization takes place with little forethought as to the culture of the institution. New faculty, for example, learn the bureaucratic procedures of when they must file particular papers and grades; but they do not learn about the ethos of their college. Institutions need to implement strategies that not only aid newcomers in functioning in a bureaucratic system, but also aid the neophyte in comprehending the cultural system as well.

Curriculum

As with the discussion about the mission, I have no intention of recommending a generic curriculum for different institutions; the point is not to substitute one cultural literacy test for another. Instead, institutions need to link their discussions about the institutional mission into their curricular affairs committees and into the classroom. This view maintains that vast possibilities exist for administrators, faculty, and students to redefine the nature of the learning experience beyond what skills are needed for the work world. Again, such discussions stem from the assumption that postsecondary education's curriculum should center on how we as citizens can develop a more just, humane, and equitable social order both within the university and in society.

By attempting such a discussion we ought to be aware of the inherent premises about the curriculum argued for in this book. In working from the assumption that a curriculum is a powerful act that structures how organizational participants think about and organize knowledge, I reject the idea that the primary purpose of a curriculum is to inculcate into youth the accumulated wisdom of society. Institutional curricula need to be investigated from the perspective of *whose* knowledge, history, language, and culture is under examination. Conversely, the organization's participants need to uncover those whose voices are *not* present in a curricular discourse and give them life.

In so doing, educators will reject the idea that knowledge is static or objective, and explore how knowledge is socially constructed. Such an investigation might revolve around questions such as:

• How do we define knowledge?
• What accounts for a knowledgeable individual?
• How has what we define as knowledge changed over time?
• Whose interests have been advanced by these forms of knowledge?
• Whose interests have been superseded or ignored by such forms?
• How do we transmit knowledge?

Further, the organization's participants need to help students see the interconnections among different courses or facets of knowledge. Too often we leave to the student the responsibility of seeing how sometimes disparate subjects connect. One way to help the student make connections across disciplines is to foster interdisciplinary coursework and an ongoing course throughout a student's career that tries to synthesize knowledge learned in other courses. It is also important to view the pedagogical methods through which an institution teaches students. Of consequence, an emancipatory view of learning affords students a greater say in their learning experiences than the view that students are learners who should have little input about what they are to learn. The ability of students to have more control over their time, to be co-learners in the learning experience, and to be able to provide assessment and feedback to other students allows for a more participatory, reflective atmosphere than the assumption that students need to acquire knowledge in order to be able to respond. The former assumption is that knowledge relates to the social contexts of the learner; whereas the latter assumption is that knowledge is an intellectual construct that teachers can give students.

Recent suggestions have been made for a "freshman-year experience" and a "senior thesis" to assess if the student is learning what he or she is supposed to learn. I am more concerned that students become aware that the synthesis of knowledge, rather than being static, is an ongoing project that demands reflection, open-mindedness, constant attention, and awareness. In this light, the importance of an honor's thesis such as the one used at Classics College is not only the *outcome*, but also the *process* of the experience itself, so that the student arrives at an understanding of how he or she has access to the tools to unearth knowledge. The goal is no longer *summative* in nature; honor's theses or similar projects are *formative*—they help focus the purpose of learning toward empowering students rather than enlightening them. What we arrive at, then, are glimpses of what a curriculum might look like that is centrally concerned with citizenship and democracy as defined by an institution's mission. Students learn about their relationship to the world as they are situated within specific discourses of power and authority.

A democratic curriculum also will have students learn to challenge dominant assumptions critically and to give life to the disempowered and dispossessed. By consistently speaking of the "disempowered" or the "voiceless," I mean to imply that the essence of a democratic society is that it celebrates the diversity of its people. Rather than assume that we should speak with one voice, a curriculum provides a forum for the many voices that account for our society. Of necessity, primacy is given to those groups whose histories have been neglected or mangled by the dominant forces at work in society. The proposition is that institutions give special attention to resurrecting those histories so that we as a nation can utilize the strength and vibrancy of all our people to the fullest extent possible.

Faculty

An overview of faculty life in these case studies paints a confusing portrait of groups and individuals being pulled in various directions— from the culture of the national system, the profession, the discipline, and the institution. Consider, for example, how faculty identify with one another as a profession. One faculty member comments about the profession by saying: "If an article comes up in *Newsweek* about colleges, sure I'll read it because it's about me. I'll probably skip the news about the refrigerator repairman's job. So I'd say I have ties to my profession.'' Recall the faculty of Working Class State College who see their ties as professional more than disciplinary or institutional in part because of the statewide collective bargaining agreement.

The discipline of a faculty member also makes demands. Faculty attend conferences and write articles; they read narrowly defined journals and converse with other faculty at other institutions who are in the same discipline. Yet the discipline also creates peculiar pressures and constraints on the faculty. Think of the typical career path of a faculty member at any of the institutions under study. Geertz elaborates:

One starts at the center of things and then moves toward the edges. Induction into the community takes place at or near the top or center. But most people are not settled at or near the top or center but at some region lower down, further out—whatever the image should be. . . . The majority of people follow a career pattern in which they are for several years at the perceived heart of things and then, in differing degrees and with different speeds, are "downwardly mobile"—or, again, at least perceive themselves to be (1983, p. 159).

And faculty act out their career patterns on the turfs of their institution's culture. What are the consequences of faculty affiliations in the profession and the discipline for the institution? As we have seen, what the institution wants from an individual or a faculty may be in conflict or competition with both the discipline and the profession. Cutting Edge College is a good example. To shun disciplinary work and tenure violates two of the major taboos of the other cultures. However, the participants within this culture have consciously chosen another path to follow. At Women's College one camp of the faculty thinks of the other camp as unable to operate within the disciplinary realm, which is why they want to change the institution's culture.

The point is not that all institutions or individuals should mindlessly break all taboos, or that professional, disciplinary, and institutional cultures must be in symbiosis with one another. Organizational participants ought to struggle to understand what the inner workings are within each culture, and what the implications are for the institution. In other words, I suggest that we imagine the work lives of faculty as individuals involved in a process that necessarily concerns cultural mores binding them to some ideas while excluding others. We need to understand which ideas bind and which exclude, and also how we might create a curriculum that transfers this understanding to students as well.

Faculty need to investigate the discourses of their lives so that they may change their realities. As with any metamorphosis, no one can predict what the change will be; however, even if faculty cannot be masters of their destinies, they can discover new ways to think about the work of their lives, and come to terms with the "master fictions" that rule. Rather than controlling their lives, faculty might try to come to terms with the nature of their habitat and decode the elements that conflict. With such understanding will come not a Prometheus unchained and unbound, but individuals whose intellectual lives are grounded in forms of moral and ethical discourse that articulate curricular possibilities for transforming not only their own culture, but also the society at large. In so doing, both the lives of faculty and the work of faculty will be to question how knowledge is produced, how it constrains and prohibits social tolerance, and under what conditions emancipatory change may take place.

For this to happen, cultural studies must offer better descriptions and analyses than the kind of superficial investigations of academic life that observe how some individuals like to deal with managers who walk around and others who do not. Cultural analyses ought to engage faculty and students in studies of the conditions under which they are produced. The goal is to develop an understanding of the discursive practices by which faculty produce and are produced by their reality. By engaging in this form of critical discourse the faculty will be interrogating their own practices as they struggle to locate a different concept of knowledge than we currently have. My assumption is that faculty as transformative leaders can create the stimulus for academic change. Since I assume that organizational life is not linear and predictable, I cannot provide a generalizable blueprint of action for faculty leaders. However, the case studies offer clues, suggestions of possible guideposts for developing a critical discourse.

Toward a Curriculum of Difference. An approach to curriculum building should allow for different voices to be heard and legitimated. As transformative leaders, faculty need to create a curriculum that uses as a basis for decision making a philosophic commitment to democracy. A democratic curriculum is built upon the fundamentals of social justice, tolerance, and a willingness to work for others rather than one's self. Such a curriculum goes beyond the notion that authors of another color or sex should be added in equal portions. A curriculum is not simply a recipe where minority voices are the "spice." The concern is not just a concern for diversity; rather, through an inclusion of multiple voices the organization's participants will be able to create conditions of a better world. To that extent, faculty need to look beyond parochial interests toward how the curriculum as an entity allows for such diversity.

Faculty as Learners. Faculty should approach students not as vessels to be filled with knowledge, but as co-learners engaged in a process of self-discovery. Students mirror faculty and institutional behaviors. Students need to see more demonstrable examples of faculty being involved with intellectual pursuits. When an institution engages in formalized meetings that focus on requirements and restrictions, or when students observe that faculty life concerns evaluating people, transformative discourse does not occur. Simply stated, to be concerned about equity and social justice, students need to hear people talking about and acting on such issues. And such concerns should occur not only in the classroom. How faculty interact with one another, how they spend their time, provides strong signals to students about the nature of academic life, and ultimately, the nature of knowledge.

Inductive Reasoning. If we are in agreement that a strictly linear, deductive model of decision making does not work, then faculty need to think how they may make decisions in a cultural organization. As transformative leaders, faculty need to develop intuitive and creative strategies rather than deductive and concrete ones. John F. Kennedy's inaugural address is an example of visionary thinking that captured the essence of where a people wanted their country to go, but the speech did not lay out step-by-step procedures for getting us there. Too often, faculty fall back into partisan curricular politics that rely on what one department will gain or lose with a particular curricular design, rather than envisioning a curriculum of possibility, of hope.

Administrators

As with the faculty, several clues exist from the case studies for academic administrators to think about as they conduct their daily affairs. Disparate perceptions arise. In many respects a key to transformative leadership concerns the engagement of these disparate perceptions. Three suggestions are offered.

Orchestrate Symbols. Organizational culture operates through human interaction and interpretation. Administrators need to determine not only the paths they wish to take, but also how the faculty will interpret such directions. Elsewhere Chaffee and I have commented that administrators should engage in "high levels of communication to convey messages about what the organization is, what is happening within and around and where it aims to go" (1988, p. 189). A critical administration recognizes that its interests do not have to compete with those of the faculty or other constituencies. However, in large part people perceive that administrators administer, teachers teach, and neither group has similar concerns. Although the clear delineation of responsibility and workload is at times necessary, administrators ought to consider alternatives to processes that serve to reproduce the workplace and instead implement forums for decision making that give expression to the multiple voices we have heard in these case studies.

Administrators need to be mindful of the way faculty lead their lives and orchestrate administrative action more toward a cultural model of the organization that emphasizes symbolic management and less toward a decision-making style that is efficient, but not efficacious. In short, academic administrators need to free themselves of those managerial tasks that constrain them into thinking about curricular issues as problems with solutions and more toward a model that suggests what the organization is about.

Administrators as Teachers. A second, ancillary suggestion is that administrators need to view their role as more educative and less managerial. Administrators ought to think of themselves as co-learners, and that essentially they too need to engage in a teaching and learning process with the faculty about the conditions of the workplace. By attempting to redefine the nature of administrative-faculty relationships I am cognizant that the current foundation upon which the relationship exists is often unhealthy and unproductive. As antagonists, faculty show disdain for managers, and administrators bemoan the muddle-headed thinking of faculty. Working from such views it is little wonder that neither group hears what the other says.

It is advocated that administrators accentuate the blurred lines of authority that exist in academe rather than clear those lines up. Rather than concentrate on structural rearrangements, administrators should become more involved in the intellectual dilemmas that confront the institution. Rather than absent themselves from curricular debate, college and university presidents ought to engage in a critical discussion about their institution's curriculum and its relationship to democracy. When administrators try to act more like managers, their actions often are of no avail. To set up decision-making committees that meet once a month where the community does not feel part of the process seems a waste of everyone's time. Instead, administrators should view their jobs more as teachers and as co-learners whose principal task is a *philosophic* one: to engage the community in a dialogue about its academic purpose.

Develop Inductive Reasoning. As with the faculty, transformative leaders need to think about the inductive side of administration and less about the deductive. Transformative leadership is premised upon the assumption that administrators will think in ways other than what it takes to accomplish a task. Rather than seek to develop styles or traits that will successfully manage people, transformative administrators seek to transform the work situation of those people with whom they operate. Such a transformation will come about by relinquishing the trappings of power and authority and empowering people to look upon themselves as leaders. In so doing, the administrator articulates for the people the visions and goals of the institution in a demonstrable manner.

By working on a cultural level along with the faculty, the administration will be reorienting the stories and ceremonies that an organization celebrates. Insofar as organizational participants live in a human world, dissonance will always occur; however, the conflict that excludes some from the discussion or creates cadres of dispossessed will be gradually acknowledged and changed. A theme that runs throughout the study of culture is the commitment to shared values. Stories and ceremonies exemplify what these values are. By orienting the work of a manager toward culture, I am highlighting the centrality of values in an organization. Further, I acknowledge that such values are not simply handed down from generation to generation, but are continually realized through organizational interaction and articulation.

In short, we must conceptualize a theory of academic administration that sees the organization as a social construction. Rather than be overly concerned with creating new markets or developing tests for student learning, the academic administrator is more of a translator who tries to interpret the organizational mission for others. The interpretation is by way of dialogue that incorporates new members' ideas and a dialogue that is done in an atmosphere that encourages democratic debate and active communication. Katz has noted that, "with few, if any, common values or shared purposes to which to appeal, only extraordinary leaders can summon the loyalty and commitment necessary to galvanize faculty sentiment around decisive, controversial, or risky actions. The result is a kind of administrative schizophrenia" (1987, p. 183).

Transformative leadership is centrally concerned with developing and maintaining the common values of an institution. Necessarily, transformative leaders must have an intimate involvement with the life of the institution. In many respects the culture of the institution will determine the form that transformative leadership takes. The academic vice president at Testimony presumably must work quietly, through consultation and a processual approach. The academic vice president at Cutting Edge has more leeway to take risks. In large part, because Entrepreneurial and Working Class have so few common values, administrative action is met with resistance.

CONCLUSION

This work has sought to portray a more complete picture of the terrain of the curriculum than we have traditionally been given. The various perceptions and attitudes of different constituencies, as they try to make sense of their lives, have been mapped from the framework of critical theory and culture. Quite often, sense-making occurs on the landscape of the curriculum. People's conception of knowledge, their perception of their role in academic life, often gets played out, distorted, uncovered, as an institution decides what it offers, what its curriculum will be. In this light people are both subjects and objects within an organization's culture. Struggle and contestation take place as the organizational participants define what their institution is about, to whom they will give voice, and whom they will keep silent.

This work has been a call to reorient our thinking about academic administration and the curriculum. It has pointed toward the notion that faculty and administrators have the ability to be transformative leaders whose central concern is how to operationalize a unique collegiate mission and put into practice strategies based on democracy and empowerment. It has consciously avoided suggesting specific decision-making structures that administrators should create to implement curricular change. Certainly, in any collegiate organization democratic procedures will necessitate bureaucratic structures. It is not suggested that anarchy should reign supreme. Decisions always need to be reached and ideas implemented; yet the processes the constituents use to reach their decisions and implement their ideas will go a long way in determining the nature of the outcomes. Without a sense of institutional purpose and commitment, as Michael Katz observes, "form triumphs over substance, practice is governed by routine, and a small number of interested people effectively exert control" (1987, p. 175).

Like mountain climbing, few rules exist that will show us the way. And like reaching a summit's peak, our struggle is not an idyll that deludes us into thinking we have reached a utopia. The view that a summit affords provides the strength to continue, to climb other mountains, to delve into other canyons where other histories wait to be unearthed and written.

Appendix: Design of the Study

A qualitative research design was devised that gave voice to different constituencies' thoughts and actions. The intent was for the interviews and observations to provide the "thick description" (Geertz, 1973) that often is lacking from quantitative surveys. This concurs with Clark's assessment of social inquiry when he wrote about his research on the faculty by saying:

> No one method of social inquiry is ideal. The approach of open-ended field interviewing on which I rely is deficient in its inability to demonstrate representativeness and in its loose control of bias in deciding what will be reported. But it is better to suffer the slings of such selection than the sorrows of superficial responses that inhere when respondents answer mail questionnaires by simply checking boxes or circling numbers opposite prepared answers, unable to explain what they individually mean, or to say what is really uppermost in their minds (1987, p. xxvi).

Thus, I set out to seven different institutions with the purpose of listening to people's stories and to find out what was "uppermost in their minds." The interviews have been quoted extensively to give the reader a sense of "being there." Some may feel that the particular has been emphasized at the expense of generalizing the findings. The intent was not to generalize. The purpose has been to highlight the differences that are at work in academe and to suggest unifying themes so that the reader can see if the differences and suggestions resonate with his or her own experiences and institutions.

INTERVIEWS AND OBSERVATIONS

The research was begun during the summer of 1987. The institutions were chosen on the basis of size, institutional diversity, and curricular offerings. As broad a sample as possible was sought, given a limited sample size.

I first set foot on the seven campuses in the early fall and returned again in the spring. After each president agreed to the study, I worked with an institutional liaison to set up the kinds of interviews and observations I wanted. Prior to each visit I studied historical documents such as the institution's history or an accreditation report. Once on campus, I interviewed as broad an array of people as possible: faculty new and old, in different disciplines, and of different races and of both sexes. Checking after the fall visits, to see which particular groups had been left out, I made a special attempt to speak with them on a return visit. At one institution, for example, in the fall I only spoke with tenured faculty. The spring visit included junior faculty. At another institution, the fall interviews took in only faculty and administrators; in the spring, students, parents, and trustees were included.

Similarly, I asked to attend meetings that pertained to the curriculum on any level—departmental, divisional, or collegewide. At one institution in the fall I attended many meetings, and at another institution, none. On returning in the spring I reversed the process. While on campus, I collected a vast array of documents—minutes of meetings, college catalogs, daily newspapers and bulletins—to name but a few—and studied documents regarding the history and present status of the colleges.

The primary focus of the research, however, was the interview. All interviews lasted at least one-half hour, and some interviews lasted for over an hour and a half. Interviews varied from one-on-one sessions to small group interviews of up to a dozen people. On the return visits, I reinterviewed some individuals and also spoke to new people. A certain calculated randomness characterized the interviews. A list submitted to the liaison at the institution of the kinds of people to be interviewed was as diverse as possible. The intent was to jog the liaison's memory so that not only those people who were either convenient or institutional allies were presented. The liaison then provided a list. Individuals recommended by others also were sought out. Using the notion of theoretical sampling introduced by Glaser and Strauss (1967) and elaborated by McLaughlin (1987), contact was also initiated with the opposites of the interviewees. After interviewing a severe critic of the curriculum at the institution, I then undertook to locate a strong supporter.

The participants themselves taught me where and what to observe, how to listen, how to ask, and how to interpret what goes on. McLaughlin notes, "The native view of reality is thus brought to bear, but only as a longitudinal learning process effected by members of the group. . . . The quest for holism derives from an interest in interpreting reality from insiders' points of view'' (1987, p. 57). Thus, the interviews were open-ended and provided individuals with the ability to respond in any number of different ways about the curriculum and their relationship to it. Over time, the open-ended questions became more selective and focused.

METHOD OF ANALYSIS

All individuals were free to refuse to be interviewed. Virtually everyone agreed, although in some instances last-minute scheduling conflicts caused a cancellation. Everyone was also promised anonymity. To protect the informants, at times the description of the data has been minimally compromised. That is, often it would help the reader to know more about a speaker than that he or she is a ''professor''; at the same time, to disclose more information might have identified the individual. If the quote were sensitive—a statement critical of the president, for example—obviously the anonymity of the individual had to be protected at the expense of ''thick description.''

Interviews were transcribed by three methods: taping, taking notes, and, on a few occasions, simply listening and writing up a short summary immediately afterwards. Different methods of transcription bring forth different kinds of data, which is one way to check on one's findings.

As time passed, patterns formed. Images and themes began to emerge from the data. A cultural approach to inquiry readily acknowledges that not only the research participants' world but also the researcher's world is socially constructed, historically determined, and based in values. ''Theory serves an agentic function, and research illustrates (vivifies) rather than provides a truth test,'' notes Lather (1986, p. 259). By rejecting the concept of ''value-free'' knowledge, I sought to expose the contradictions at work in everyday life. In so doing the work demanded an analysis that investigated not only the grand changes that took place, such as a faculty overhaul of the curriculum, but also the petty, mundane activities that mark our existence in the workplace. From the analysis and description of the contradictions that operate in postsecondary organizations, we are better able to grasp the reality of the participants and, of consequence, suggest avenues for change or improvement.

Given the theoretical nature of this work, it seems appropriate to point out how my ideas changed during the course of the research and how I insured that the conclusions ultimately reached derived from the data and were not merely personally opined conclusions. As long ago as 1922, Malinowski observed that a researcher should not enter the field ''determined to prove a hypothesis'' (p. 8). I had no hypotheses to prove, but I did have ideas about the curriculum and the nature of higher education, set forth in Part I. My purpose was to provide vivid descriptions of organizational life and how power, authority, ideology, and culture exist and operate within the organization.

At the outset of the research I had few, if any, ideas about what I would find at the specific research sites. Nevertheless, traveling to a research site one always wonders, "What will it be like?" Over time, as I contextualized the data, it was a surprise to find, for example, similarities between Christian University and its most liberal counterpart, Cutting Edge College. The degree of curricular rigidity uncovered at Classics College was unexpected. How to interpret the goings-on at Entrepreneurial College was at first baffling. My ideas similarly changed as I gathered more data and listened to more people.

Lather (1986) proposes four guidelines for guarding against researcher bias: triangulation, face validity, catalytic validity, and construct validity. In *triangulating* data I used multiple data sources and employed a variety of methodological devices such as interviews, observations, and historical analyses.

Face validity concerns what Guba and Lincoln (1981) call "member checks." It involves confronting the respondents with one's findings and refining one's results in light of the respondents' concerns. I gave this document to all of the institutional liaisons and received feedback and comments from some. Their comments and advice helped further refine the data and analysis. Some of the liaisons shared the book with other interested individuals. Their comments also helped to change some of the initial findings. While on campus I talked with interviewees about some of my preliminary findings; they enlightened me when I was on the right track, or unburdened me of a false idea when I had not listened well enough. Midway through the project I presented some initial ideas to my colleagues at a small higher-education conference on leadership at Princeton. Many conversations with individuals at the conference provided insights about different ways to think about the data.

Catalytic validity "refers to the degree to which the research process reorients, focuses, and energizes participants in what Freire (1970) calls 'conscientization' knowing reality in order to better transform it" (Lather, 1986, p. 67). Whether I have been successful in employing this concept is yet to be seen. After interviews and, occasionally, months afterward in letters, respondents have commented that the ability to reflect on the questions raised in a nonjudgmental atmosphere helped them to reconceptualize their own thinking about the curriculum. My hope is that this document will eventually work its way around the campuses I studied and will be a talking piece for them. But catalytic validity is a process that takes much longer than the formal length of a research agenda; it is an ongoing process. In many respects a goal of this book is to help "conscientization" take place.

Construct validity is the final guideline offered. The concern with this concept is to be able to show how one's a priori theory has changed during the research process. Indeed, one may well wonder how the collection of all this data changed my own ideas about the curriculum. The simplest answer is that when this project began the working title for this book was *Academic Leadership and Managing the Curriculum*. By listening to and observing individuals, however, I realized the futility in thinking that anyone can "manage" the curriculum. As a social construct, the curriculum is too malleable to manage: American higher education needs more than simply "academic leadership"; we need a visionary kind of leadership that speaks for all people, not only those who reside in the upper echelons of the administration. I had not realized the degree to which people desired to understand the meanings of their institutions. Thus, we see how different the results of this project are from its genesis. My hope is that people will take the words, voices, and ideas generated in this work and debate the concepts in their own institutions as we move toward revising and reforming the curriculum for the twenty-first century.

References

Albert, S., & Whetten, D. (1985). Organizational identity. *Research in Organizational Behavior*, 7, 263–295.

Apple, M. W. (1986). *Teachers and texts: A political economy of class and gender relations in education*. New York, NY: Routledge & Kegan Paul.

Aronowitz, S. & Giroux, H. (1985). *Education under siege: The conservative, liberal, and radical debate over schooling*. South Hadley, MA: Bergin & Garvey Publishers, Inc.

Aronowitz, S. (1985). Academic freedom: A structural approach. *Educational Theory*, 35(1), 1–13.

Association of American Colleges. (1985). *Integrity in the college curriculum: A report to the academic community*. Washington, DC: Association of American Colleges.

Bell, D. (1967). Reforming general education. In C. Lee (Ed.), *Improving college teaching*. Washington, DC: American Council on Education.

Bennett, J. B. (1983). *Managing the academic department, cases and notes*. New York, NY: ACE/Macmillan.

Bennett, W. J. (1984). *To reclaim a legacy: A report on the humanities in higher education*. Washington, DC: National Endowment for the Humanities.

Bennis, W. (1984). Transformative power and leadership. In T. Sergiovanni & J. Corbally (Eds.), *Leadership and organizational culture: New perspectives on administrative theory and practice*, 64–71. Urbana, IL: University of Illinois Press.

Bergquist, W. (1977). Eight curricular models. In A. Chickering, et al. (Eds.), *Developing the college curriculum*. Washington, DC: Council for the Advancement of Small Colleges.

Birnbaum, R. (1988). *How colleges work*. San Francisco, CA: Jossey-Bass.

Bloom, A. (1987). *The closing of the American mind*. New York, NY: Simon and Schuster.

Bourdieu, P. (1981). Men and machines. In K. Knorr-Cetina & A. Cicourel (Eds.), *Advances in social method and methodology*. Boston, MA: Routledge & Kegan Paul.

Bourdieu, P. (1977). *Outline of a theory of practice*. Cambridge: Cambridge University Press.

Boyer, E. (1987). *College: The undergraduate experience in America*. New York, NY: Harper & Row.

Brown, D. (Ed.). (1984). *Leadership roles of chief academic officers. New Directions for Higher Education*, 47. San Francisco, CA: Jossey-Bass.

Burgess, D. (1952). *Dream and deed: The story of Katharine Lee Bates*. Tulsa, OK: University of Oklahoma Press.

Burns, J. (1978). *Leadership*. New York, NY: Harper & Row.

Cameron, K., & Ulrich, D. (1986). Transformational leadership. In J. Smart, *Higher education: Handbook of theory and research*, 1–42. New York, NY: Agathon Press.

Chaffee, E. (1984). Successful strategic management in small private colleges. *Journal of Higher Education*, 55(2), 212–241.

Chaffee, E., & Tierney, W. G. (1988). *Collegiate culture and leadership strategy*. New York, NY: Macmillan.

Chait, R. (1979). Mission madness strikes our colleges. *The Chronicle of Higher Education*, 18(36), 36.

Chickering, A., Halliburton, D., Bergquist, W., & Lindquist, J. (1977). *Developing the college curriculum: A handbook for faculty and administrators*. Washington, DC: Council for the Advancement of Small Colleges.

Clark, B. (1987). *The academic life*. Princeton, NJ: The Carnegie Foundation for the Advancement of Teaching.

Clark, B. (1983). *The higher education system: Academic organization in cross-national perspective*. Berkeley, CA: University of California Press.

Clark, B. (1980). The organizational saga in higher education. In H. Leavitt (Ed.), *Readings in managerial psychology*. Chicago, IL: Chicago University Press.

Clark, B. (1971). Belief and loyalty in college organization. *Journal of Higher Education*, 42, 499–520.

Cohen, M., & March, J. (1974). *Leadership and ambiguity: The American college president*. New York, NY: McGraw-Hill.

Cohen, M., March, J., & Olsen, J. (1972). A garbage can model of organizational choice. *Administrative Science Quarterly*, 17(1), 1–25.

Commission for Educational Quality. (1985). *Access to quality undergraduate education.* Atlanta, GA: Southern Region Education Board.

Conrad, C. (Ed.). (1985). *ASHE reader on academic programs in colleges and universities.* Washington, DC: Association for the Study of Higher Education.

Davies, G. K. (1986). The importance of being general: Philosophy, politics, and institutional mission statements. In J. Smart (Ed.), *Higher Education: Handbook of Theory and Research, Volume II.* New York, NY: Agathon Press.

Deal, T., & Kennedy, A. (1982). *Corporate cultures: The rites and rituals of corporate life.* Reading, MA: Addison-Wesley.

Dewey, J. (1963). *Experience and education.* New York, NY: Macmillan.

Dressel, P. (1971). *College and university curriculum.* Berkeley, CA: McCutchan.

El-Khawas, E. (1987). *Campus trends, 1987. Higher Education Panel Reports,* #75. Washington, DC: American Council on Education.

Ehrle, E., & Bennett, J. (1988). *Managing the academic enterprise.* New York, NY: Macmillan.

Foster, W. (1986). *Paradigms and promises: New approaches to educational administration.* Buffalo, NY: Prometheus Books.

Freire, P. (1970). *Pedagogy of the oppressed.* New York, NY: Seabury Press.

Foucault, M. (1980). *Power/knowledge.* New York, NY: Pantheon.

Foucault, M. (1978). *The history of sexuality.* New York, NY: Pantheon.

Foucault, M. (1972). *The archaeology of knowledge.* New York, NY: Pantheon.

Geertz, C. (1973). *The interpretation of cultures.* New York, NY: Basic Books.

Geertz, C. (1983). *Local knowledge.* New York, NY: Basic Books.

Giroux, H. A. (1987). Citizenship, public philosophy, and the struggle for democracy. *Educational Theory*, 37(2), 103–120.

Giroux, H. A. (1986). Authority, intellectuals, and the politics of practical learning. *Teachers College Record*, 88(1), 22–40.

Giroux, H. A. (1983). *Theory & resistance in education: A pedagogy for the opposition.* South Hadley, MA: Bergin & Garvey.

Giroux, H. A., & McLaren, P. (1986). Teacher education and the politics of engagement: The case for democratic schooling. *Harvard Educational Review*, 56(3), 213–238.

Glaser, B., & Strauss, A. (1967). *Discovery of grounded theory: Strategies for qualitative research.* Chicago, IL: Aldine.

Gould, J. W. (1964). *The academic deanship.* New York, NY: Teachers College, Columbia University.

Graff, G. (1988). Conflicts over the curriculum are here to stay; they should be made educationally productive. *The Chronicle of Higher Education*, February 17, 1988.

Guba, E., & Lincoln, Y. (1981). *Effective evaluation*. San Francisco, CA: Jossey-Bass.

Gudykunst, W. (1985). Normative power and conflict potential in intergroup relationships. In W. Gudykunst, L. Stewart, & S. Ting-Toomey (Eds.), *Communication, culture, and organizational processes*. Beverly Hills, CA: Sage.

Hefferlin, L. (1969). *Dynamics of academic reform*. San Francisco, CA: Jossey-Bass.

Hirsch, E. (1987).*Cultural literacy: What every American needs to know*. Boston, MA: Houghton-Mifflin.

Hirsch, P., & Andrews, J. (1983). Ambushes, shootouts, and knights of the roundtable: The language of corporate takeovers. In L. Pondy, P. Frist, G. Morgan, & T. Dandridge (Eds.), *Organizational symbolism*, 145–155. Greenwich, CT: JAI Press.

Holland, J. R. (1985). A nation at risk. *The Review of Higher Education*, 9(1), 51–65.

Hutchins, R. M. (1936). *The higher learning in America*. New Haven, CT: Yale University Press.

Jacoby, R. (1987). *The last intellectuals: American culture in the age of academe*. New York, NY: Basic Books.

Katz, M. B. (1987). *Reconstructing American education*. Cambridge, MA: Harvard University Press.

Keller, G. (1985). Trees without fruit. *Change*, January/February, 7–10.

Keller, G. (1983). *Academic strategy: The management revolution in American higher education*. Baltimore, MD: Johns Hopkins University Press.

Kerr, C., & Gade, M. (1987). The contemporary college president. *The American Scholar*, 29–44.

Krakower, J. Y. (1985). *Assessing organizational effectiveness: Considerations and procedures*. Boulder, CO: National Center for Higher Education Management Systems.

Kuh, G., & Whitt, E. (1988). Using the cultural lens to understand faculty behavior. Paper presented at the annual meeting of the American Educational Research Association, New Orleans, Louisiana.

Lather, P. (1986). Issues of validity in openly ideological research: Between a rock and a soft place. *Interchange*, 17(4), 63–84.

Lee. C. (Ed.). (1967). *Improving college teaching*. Washington, DC: American Council on Education.

Lincoln, Y. S. (1988). The role of ideology in naturalistic research. Paper presented at the annual meeting of the American Educational Research Association, New Orleans, Louisiana.

Lister, R., & Lister, F. (1981). *Chaco canyon*. Albuquerque, NM: University of New Mexico Press.

Malinowski, B. (1922). *Argonauts of the western Pacific*. London, England: Routledge.

March, J. (1984). How we talk and how we act: Administrative theory and administrative life. In T. Sergiovanni & J. Corbally, *Leadership and organizational culture*, 18–35. Urbana, IL: University of Illinois Press.

March, J. (1978). Bounded rationality, ambiguity, and the engineering of choice. *Bell Journal of Economics*, 9, 587–608.

March, J., & Olsen, J. (1979). *Ambiguity and choice in organizations*. Bergen, Norway: *Universitetsforlaget*.

Masland, A. T. (1985). Organizational culture in the study of higher education. *The Review of Higher Education*, 8(2), 157–168.

Mayhew, L., & Ford, P. (1971). *Changing the curriculum*. San Francisco, CA: Jossey-Bass.

McLaren, P. (1986). *Schooling as a ritual performance*. London, England: Routledge.

McLaughlin, D. (1987). When literacy empowers: An ethnography of uses for English and Navajo print. Unpublished doctoral dissertation, The University of New Mexico.

Mortimer, K. P. (1986). Beyond the quality reports: Future directions and alternatives. Paper presented at the annual meeting of the Association of Institutional Research, Orlando, Florida.

Mortimer, K. P., & Caruso, A. (1984). The process of academic governance and the painful choices of the 1980s. In D. Brown (Ed.), *Leadership roles of chief academic officers, New Directions for Higher Education*, 47. San Francisco, CA: Jossey-Bass.

Mortimer, K. P. (1984a). *Involvement in learning*. Washington, DC: National Institute of Education.

Mortimer, K. P., & Tierney, M. L. (1979). *The three r's of the eighties: Reduction, reallocation, and retrenchment*. Washington, DC: American Association for Higher Education.

National Governor's Association. (1986). *Time for results*. Washington, DC: National Governor's Association.

Newman, F. (1985). *Higher education and the American resurgence*. New York, NY: Carnegie Foundation for the Advancement of Teaching.

Nyberg, D., & Farber, P. (1986). Authority in education. *Teachers College Record*, 88(1), 4–14.

Peck, R. D. (1984). Entrepreneurship as a significant factor in successful adaptation. *Journal of Higher Education*, 55(2), 269–285.

Peters, T., & Waterman, R. (1982). *In search of excellence*. New York, NY: Harper & Row.

Pfeffer, J. (1981). Management as symbolic action: The creation and maintenance of organizational paradigms. In L. Cummings & B. Staw, *Research in organizational behavior*. Greenwich, CT: JAI Press.

Rudolph, F. (1985). *Integrity in the college curriculum: A report to the academic
community*. Washington, DC: Association of American Colleges.

Rudolph, F. (1977). *Curriculum: A history of the American undergraduate
course of study since 1636*. San Francisco, CA: Jossey-Bass.

Schein, E. H. (1985). *Organizational culture and leadership*. San Francisco,
CA: Jossey-Bass.

Schuh, G. E. (1986). Revitalizing land-grant universities. *Choices*, Second
Quarter, 6–10.

Schuster, M., & Van Dyne, S. (1984). Placing women in the liberal arts: Stages
of curriculum transformation. *Harvard Educational Review*, 54(4), 413–
428.

Scott, W. R. (1981). *Organizations: Rational, natural, and open systems*. En-
glewood Cliffs, NJ: Prentice-Hall.

Siegel, H. (1987). Rationality and ideology. *Educational Theory*, 37(2), 153–
167.

Simon, R., & Dippo, D. (1986). On critical ethnographic work. *Anthropology
and Education Quarterly*, 17(34), 195–202.

Sinclair, U. (1923). *The goose step*. KS: Haldeman Publications.

Smith, J. K. (1988). Looking for the easy way out: The desire for methodological constraints in openly ideological inquiry. Paper presented at the
annual meeting of the American Educational Research Association, New
Orleans, Louisiana.

Sypher, B., Applegate, J., & Sypher, H. (1985). Culture and communication
in organizational contexts. In W. Gudykunst, L. Stewart, & S. Ting-
Toomey (Eds.), *Communication, culture, and organizational processes*,
13–29. Beverly Hills, CA: Sage.

Tierney, W. G. (1989). Symbolism and presidential perceptions of leadership.
Review of Higher Education, 12(2), 153–166.

Tierney, W. G. (1988a). Organizational culture in higher education: Defining
the essentials. *Journal of Higher Education*, 59(1), 2–21.

Tierney, W. G. (1988). *The web of leadership: The presidency in higher education*. Greenwich, CT: JAI Press.

Tierney, W. G. (1987). Facts and constructs: Defining reality in higher education organizations. *Review of Higher Education*, 11(1), 61–73.

Trice, H., & Beyer, J. (1984). Studying organizational cultures through rites
and ceremonials. *The Academy of Management Review*, 9(4), 653–669.

Tucker, A. (1984). *Chairing the academic department: Leadership among
peers*. New York, NY: ACE/Macmillan.

Veblen, T. (1957). *The higher learning in America*. New York, NY: Hill and
Wang.

Weick, K. E. (1976). Educational organizations as loosely coupled systems. *Administrative Science Quarterly*, 21(1), 1–19.

Weis, L. (1985). Faculty perspectives and practice in an urban community college. *Higher Education*, 14, 553–574.

Whitman, W. (1949). *Democratic vistas*. New York, NY: Liberal Arts Press. Originally published 1871.

Willis, P. (1977). *Learning to labor: How working class kids get working class jobs*. New York, NY: Columbia University Press.

Wolff, R. P. (1969). *The ideal of the university*. Boston, MA: Beacon Press.

Zammuto, R. F. (1986). Managing decline in American higher education. In J. Smart (Ed.), *Higher education: Handbook of theory and research, Volume II*. New York, NY: Agathon Press.

Zavarzadeh, M., & Morton, D. (1987). War of the words: The battle of (and for) English. *In These Times*, October/November, 18–19.

Index

ABOUT THE AUTHOR

WILLIAM G. TIERNEY is a Senior Research Associate and Associate Professor at the Center for the Study of Higher Education at Penn State University. Tierney holds an advanced degree in anthropology, a doctorate in education from Stanford University, and an advanced degree in education from Harvard University. He is the author of *The Web of Leadership* and *Collegiate Culture and Leadership Strategies* (with Ellen Chaffee). Tierney brings with him both administrative experience as an academic dean at a Native American community college and ethnographic insight from Peace Corps work in Morocco. He is an avid long-distance runner and mountain climber.